"Rhiannon's book will be so helpful for neurodivergent teens! It is built on a framework of neurodiversity-affirming care and compassion, which is so critical to helping youth develop the self-validation and advocacy skills they need. The book contains nonjudgmental, non-pathologized descriptions of various aspects of a neurodiverse brain and nervous system, and I love the emphasis on helping kids think about themselves and their goals through a neurodiversity-affirming framework."

—*Lorie Ritschel, PhD*, expert dialectical behavior therapy (DBT) trainer and consultant, associate professor of psychiatry at UNC School of Medicine, and co-owner of Triangle Area Psychology Clinic

"*The Neurodivergence Skills Workbook for Teens* distills DBT skills into practical action steps, with examples designed to address the specific emotional, sensorial, and interpersonal experiences of neurodivergent youth. Using clear and accessible writing, Theurer nonjudgmentally maintains a neuro-affirming stance of warm acceptance, while at the same time guiding readers in enacting values-consistent changes toward building meaningful and fulfilling lives against the backdrop of a neurotypical world."

—*Sara Schmidt, PhD*, owner of Middle Path Solutions, and DBT-Linehan board-certified clinician

"Finally! A workbook that centers the experiences of neurodivergent teens! Rhiannon expertly introduces foundational concepts of neurodiversity, while creating an easily accessible balance of psychoeducation, sensory needs, strategy, and tangible tools. The finishing touch of including detailed stories made every concept incredibly relatable. I'm thrilled to share this resource with my teen clients!"

—*Jamie D. Roberts, MA, LMFT*, director of NeuroPebble Corp, founder of Equilibrium Counseling Services, and author of *Mindfulness for Teen Anxiety* and *Neurodiversity for Teen Girls*

"The encouragement to honor one's neurodivergent identity and advocate for themselves is a key feature throughout this manual. I believe this work will help reduce the gap in services provided to neurodivergent individuals by providers. The skills and assignments are easy to follow with clear, concise instructions and a variety of ways to engage with each topic. I am excited to use this manual in my clinical practice."

—*Sheena Beach, MSW, LCSW, LISW-CP*, Behavioral Tech DBT Intensively Trained Therapist, and DBT Team Lead

"Theurer's book does a wonderful job of challenging misconceptions about neurodivergence, and represents a range of experiences for teens that they can relate to. This workbook provides affirming context to nuanced daily living and explains DBT skills in an easy, conversational manner. I can see many clients in therapy who would greatly benefit from using the skills in this book."

—*Diadra Smith, LCSW*, neurodivergent mental health advocate, and founder of Soft Edges Therapy

THE NEURODIVERGENCE SKILLS WORKBOOK FOR TEENS

DBT TOOLS TO HELP YOU DEAL WITH SENSORY SENSITIVITY, MANAGE EMOTIONAL OVERWHELM & THRIVE

RHIANNON THEURER, LMFT

Instant Help Books

An Imprint of New Harbinger Publications, Inc.

Publisher's Note

This publication is designed to provide accurate and authoritative information in regard to the subject matter covered. It is sold with the understanding that the publisher is not engaged in rendering psychological, financial, legal, or other professional services. If expert assistance or counseling is needed, the services of a competent professional should be sought.

INSTANT HELP, the Clock Logo, and NEW HARBINGER are trademarks of New Harbinger Publications, Inc.

New Harbinger Publications is an employee-owned company.

Copyright © 2025 by Rhiannon Theurer
Instant Help Books
An imprint of New Harbinger Publications, Inc.
5720 Shattuck Avenue
Oakland, CA 94609
www.newharbinger.com

All Rights Reserved

Cover design by Amy Shoup

Interior design by Tom Comitta

Acquired by Jess O'Brien

Edited by Jennifer Holder

Library of Congress Cataloging-in-Publication Data on file

Printed in the United States of America

27 26 25
10 9 8 7 6 5 4 3 2 1   First Printing

CONTENTS

FOREWORD VII

INTRODUCTION IX

PART 1: UNDERSTANDING NEURODIVERGENCE 1

1. WHAT IS NEURODIVERGENCE? 3

2. NEURODIVERGENCE: DISABILITY OR DIFFERENCE? 8

3. WHAT IS DBT AND HOW CAN IT HELP? 12

4. SENSITIVITY 17

5. INTENSITY 22

6. EFFECTIVENESS 26

7. COGNITIVE FLEXIBILITY 29

8. EXECUTIVE FUNCTIONING 34

9. DEMAND AVOIDANCE 42

PART 2: TAKING CARE OF YOURSELF 49

10. SELF-VALIDATION 51

11. IDENTIFYING YOUR VALUES 55

12. REDUCING VULNERABILITY FACTORS 60

13. REFILLING YOUR TANK 63

14. SENSORY SYSTEMS AND REGULATION STRATEGIES 67

15. SPECIAL INTERESTS 73

16. MASKING 75

PART 3: MINDFULNESS SKILLS 81

17. STATES OF MIND 83

18. MINDFULNESS AS A NEURODIVERGENT PERSON 89

19. OBSERVE AND DESCRIBE 93

20. SENSORY-FOCUSED MINDFULNESS PRACTICES 96

21. RADICAL ACCEPTANCE 99

PART 4: RIDING THE WAVES OF EMOTION 105

22. APPRECIATING EMOTIONS 107

23. WHAT EMOTION AM I FEELING? 111

24. WORKING WITH EMOTIONS 116

25. PROBLEM SOLVE OR ACT OPPOSITE 122

26. COPING THROUGH STRONG EMOTIONS 128

27. REJECTION SENSITIVITY 136

PART 5: COMMUNICATION AND RELATIONSHIPS 141

28. NEURODIVERGENT COMMUNICATION IN A NEUROTYPICAL WORLD 143

29. SHARING YOUR NEURODIVERGENCE 147

30. BOUNDARIES 151

31. NAVIGATING CONFLICT 155

32. VALIDATING OTHERS 160

FINDING YOUR NEXT STEPS: LIVING THE LIFE YOU WANT 165

ACKNOWLEDGMENTS 169

BIBLIOGRAPHY 170

FOREWORD

In the past few decades, we have witnessed an incredible evolution in our understanding of neurodivergence. What was once marginalized or misunderstood is now increasingly recognized as a vital expression of human diversity. We have begun to embrace the idea that brains, like ecosystems, thrive in variety—and that difference is not a deficiency, but an integral part of our shared humanity.

Within the mental health field, we are slowly catching on. We are beginning to talk about autism, ADHD, sensitivity, and intensity through an identity-based framework rather than a deficit model. At the same time, we are learning more about the unique mental health needs of neurodivergent people. However, gaps remain. For example, while we know that many autistic and ADHD teens struggle with anxiety, depression, self-harm, and elevated risks of eating disorders and substance use, the field still lags in adapting treatments to address these complex needs effectively.

As an autistic ADHD psychologist, a professional in this space, and the mother of neurodivergent teenagers, I see daily the interplay between these shifting paradigms and the deeply personal struggles of our youth. Neurodivergent teens are navigating a world that is slowly waking up to their needs, yet they contend with mental health challenges shaped by neurological vulnerabilities, societal expectations, systemic inadequacies, and internalized misunderstandings. Many typical mental health approaches are complicated further by a lack of understanding of neurodivergent brain styles, such as alexithymia, sensory needs, and intensity.

That is why this book is so timely and such a welcome addition to the field. It offers both a compassionate framework for understanding the neurodivergent experience and a practical guide to supporting mental health in meaningful ways. This book serves two critical purposes: first, introducing readers to their brain style, and second, providing actionable strategies for managing vulnerabilities.

Rhiannon Theurer strikes a delicate balance in this work. She affirms neurodivergent identities and celebrates the strengths of neurodivergent brains while not shying away from the real struggles teens face. Her approach is grounded in mindfulness, emotional resilience, and interpersonal effectiveness, consistently emphasizing the importance of aligning interventions with each person's goals and values.

As I read through this book, I reflected on the neurodivergent teens I've worked with—their remarkable creativity, emotional depth, and resilience in the face of a world not yet built for them. This book felt like the resource I've longed to hand them.

I am thrilled to see this work come into existence. It is both a toolkit and a source of hope, empowering teens, their families, and their allies to embrace difference, navigate challenges with greater confidence, and build lives grounded in connection and authenticity.

My hope is that this book helps you feel deeply seen, not just in your struggles but in your strengths. May it guide you toward understanding yourself more fully and equip you with tools to move through the world in a way that feels aligned with who you are.

Dr. Megan Anna Neff
Clinical psychologist and founder of Neurodivergent Insights

INTRODUCTION

The concept of neurodivergence has recently gained popularity. People all over are becoming aware that there are different types of brains, and that those differences have been wrongly pathologized. The neurodiversity-affirming movement challenges us to look at differences between brains as neutral rather than "good" or "bad."

Whether you are new to the idea of neurodivergence or have been active in online communities for years, it's worth starting this book with the basics, to ground ourselves in the ways this book discusses neurodivergence. In the first part of this book, we'll explore commonalities of neurodivergent experience and reflect on ways these traits might show up in your life, regardless of whether you identify with a particular form of neurodivergence.

In the second part, we'll dive into how to best support your unique needs. Often, neurodivergent people have been shamed out of acknowledging their needs, much less meeting them. Yet denying your needs doesn't make them disappear.

Part 3 of this book focuses on mindfulness skills—important for all humans! Being mindful allows us to see what is actually happening in front of us. Mindfulness makes all the other practices in this book much easier as well.

In part 4, we'll look at emotions: how to recognize and understand them. Being a teenager is challenging enough emotionally, and neurodivergence often adds its own complexity to emotions. These skills will get you through even the most challenging of moments.

Part 5 is focused on communication. We'll push back on seeing neurodivergent communication styles as flawed while acknowledging that most of us benefit from skills that let us communicate more effectively with others. We'll look at how you can use these skills without invalidating yourself.

As you read, you may wish to go back and reread other sections. For example, once you know your sensory processing profile, it will be easier to track emotions. When you practice mindfulness skills, it will help with understanding your sensory style, as well as your emotions. Learning more about your emotions will help you better identify what boundaries you need, and so on.

PART 1

UNDERSTANDING NEURODIVERGENCE

SECTION 1
WHAT IS NEURODIVERGENCE?

J is fourteen. They are an artist and a gamer, and love skateboarding. They just started ninth grade at a large high school, and it's a lot. J has sensory sensitivities that make it challenging to be in loud places with a lot of people. When they're in art class or with their friends at lunch, they have ways to cope. Hallways and locker rooms, though, are a different story.

Eliot is obsessed with the Roman Empire—especially ancient Roman architecture, engineering, and military feats. When he graduates in a couple of years, his dream is to spend a summer traveling in Europe to visit the sites he's read about. Eliot is autistic, and he's only comfortable eating a few foods. He worries this will make travel impossible.

Ayesha is a talented clarinet player who expresses deep emotions in her music. She gets lost in the complexities of jazz. Her family jokes she's a pet psychic because she always seems to know what their dog is feeling. She sometimes thinks she knows too much about what everyone around her is feeling too. It can be exhausting to be so tuned in to other people.

J, Eliot, and Ayesha, like millions of teens, have their strengths and also their struggles. Also like many other teens, they are *neurodivergent*, meaning that their brains work differently in some ways than their peers' brains. Sometimes those differences show up in neurodivergent teens' strengths, and sometimes those differences seem to bring a little too much struggle. Maybe you can relate. You likely picked up this book or were handed it because you know or suspect that you are neurodivergent. In any case, welcome.

There are many ways to be neurodivergent—that is, there are a lot of different types of brains, or *neurotypes*. The existence of that variety is also known as *neurodiversity*. While no one book could address them all, this workbook will look at experiences that are common to many neurodivergent people. These include high sensitivity, intense feelings, sensory differences, attention differences, and more.

In this workbook, I hope to help you:

- reflect on your experiences

- develop a positive identity around your neurodivergence

- identify ways to advocate for your needs

We'll start by looking at what neurodiversity and neurodivergence actually mean. Then, we'll introduce some of the ideas that will help you understand your neurodivergence. These include:

- emotion regulation

- sensitivity

- intensity

- effectiveness

- executive functioning

Each section of the workbook has activities that are designed to help you explore and appreciate your neurodivergence, and practice skills that will help you enjoy life more.

You can and should engage with these prompts however you like: writing, drawing, talking to a trusted person, creating private audio files, or any other way that works best for your processing style!

NEURODIVERGENCE 101

It's a basic biological fact that there is enormous diversity among human brains. This diversity of brains, or neurodiversity, is good for our species, much as a diverse ecosystem is healthier, more robust, and just plain more interesting. While there may be advantages or disadvantages to a particular neurotype (type of brain) in a particular situation or environment, the neurotypes themselves are not inherently good or bad. For example, while dyslexia is most strongly associated in our culture with challenges with reading and writing, dyslexic brains tend to excel at spatial reasoning, which is an advantage in engineering or architecture.

Being neurodivergent simply means having a brain that works differently from how the majority of brains work, particularly when it comes to interacting with our environments and with other people. Most cultures are built around various strengths of *neurotypical* brains—brains that are not neurodivergent—and people expect behaviors that come easily to neurotypical brains. For example, in the mainstream culture of the United States, we tend to assume that:

- eye contact indicates someone is listening

- people can sit still and engage in focused work for long periods of time

- a person's mood or emotions will be fairly stable day to day

- people will be able to follow and engage in a group conversation where the discussion casually switches between topics

People who are able to follow social and behavioral expectations like these without getting overly stressed usually have neurotypical brains. People who stress about these expectations and need support are usually neurodivergent.

Sometimes, neurodivergence is used as a synonym for autism or attention-deficit/hyperactivity disorder (ADHD). But this definition is too limited. Neurodivergence can be:

- innate (something you are born with), such as autism, Down syndrome, or high sensitivity

- acquired (developing later in life), such as post-traumatic stress disorder (PTSD), social anxiety, or traumatic brain injury

- lifelong, such as ADHD, bipolar disorder, or most innate neurodivergences

- temporary, such as a depressive episode that resolves after treatment

- diagnosed by a professional

- self-identified

- noticeable to observers

- invisible to observers

Neurodivergence can involve a mental health or brain-based condition. Neurodivergence also describes types of brains that are not discussed in *The Diagnostic and Statistical Manual of Mental Disorders, Fifth Edition*, or *DSM-5* (the handbook used to diagnose mental health conditions), like giftedness or high sensitivity.

FOR YOU TO DO

Are there ways in which you are neurodivergent or suspect that you are?

What are your hopes in exploring this topic?

What are your concerns or worries in exploring this topic?

TALKING ABOUT IDENTITY

In this workbook, I use "autistic" instead of "person-first language," such as "person with autism." Person-first language aims to show a person is more than just their medical condition. For example, saying "person with diabetes" reminds us that diabetes is one part of that person's life. This is common practice for many disabilities and medical conditions. In contrast, many autistic advocates and supporters do not use person-first language. They see autism as an identity to be celebrated, not a medical condition to be treated. Many advocates also like simply using the word autism instead of phrases like "on the spectrum." Some autistic people disagree with this and prefer person-first language. It is important to respect the words people use to describe themselves. Autism is not a bad word to be avoided.

Another neurotype that faces some disagreement about language is ADHD. Some ADHD advocates point out that the term ADHD is too focused on perceived problems—the first D stands for "deficit," after all. Currently there is no widely accepted alternative name for ADHD, so I use terms like "ADHDer" throughout this book. The future may bring us other neuroaffirming language.

SECTION 2

NEURODIVERGENCE: DISABILITY OR DIFFERENCE?

Neurodivergence has often been seen as a disability. It is true that some people can feel disabled by aspects of their neurodivergence. Neurodivergence and disability are not synonymous, but attitudes toward disability often affect how we see neurodivergence.

There are two ways of seeing disability:

- The *medical model*, which looks at what is "wrong" with a person, and often focuses on finding a cure.

- The *social model*, which looks at things like physical barriers and social expectations as the cause of limitations. For example, needing to move your body while you study is only a problem if you are expected to sit in your chair quietly.

Both views of disability can be useful. Some experiences are painful, and it is understandable that people would like to not have them. For example, panic attacks are overwhelming and scary. This is true even when family, friends, and schools are supportive. A teen with panic attacks might have a *504 plan*—a plan that ensures a child with a disability receives necessary accomodations at school—that allows them to leave class and go to the counseling center when having a panic attack (social model). They also will probably want to seek treatment, such as therapy or medication, to reduce or eliminate the panic attacks (medical model). Some people may choose to engage with only the medical model or only the social model. Ideally, each person will choose the supports and treatments that meet their own goals.

Eliot wants to increase his comfort with eating. Seeing an occupational therapist is one way he uses the medical model to help himself meet this goal. Notice that he doesn't set a goal of "seeming neurotypical." When he uses his phone to text instead of using verbal speech, he uses a social strategy. Despite using the medical model, Eliot isn't treating his autism as "disordered." The therapist's services simply help him meet his goals.

Eliot engages with the medical model for his goal of increasing the number of safe foods he has. However, he does not have the goal of having no sensory sensitivities at all. Eliot draws upon the social model by using his phone to help with communication when verbal speech becomes difficult. He does not force himself to communicate in a way that could be very upsetting for him. Though he is using services in the medical model, Eliot is not stating he is "wrong" for being autistic. These services are simply used to meet goals that are important to Eliot.

Negative beliefs about disability are called *ableism*. This includes the belief that disabled people are bad or not as good as more abled people (meaning people who are not disabled). Individuals can also experience internalized ableism, or ableism directed at oneself. This can look like shame or self-hatred. Sometimes people refuse to acknowledge their need for supports, and it leads to burnout or injury. Disability is a common human experience. There is nothing wrong with being disabled or neurodivergent, even if it is challenging at times.

J refers to their sensitivities as "me just being a baby." J pushes themself to go to parties "like a normal person," even though it leaves them exhausted. J's sister sends them some YouTube videos where people talk about their sensory needs with self-acceptance. After watching the videos, J experiments with using earplugs at noisy events. J's sister also suggests doing some study groups at the library instead of going to a busy coffee shop. Since making these adjustments, J has felt better able to be more present when going out with friends.

FOR YOU TO DO

Are there challenges you face in daily functioning, whether sensory, cognitive, or emotional? If yes, what are those challenges?

How can you be better supported, using the social model of disability (supports, accommodations, environmental adaptations)?

Which of these challenges are better supported through the medical model (medication, professional services)?

Does the idea of disability as neutral raise strong emotions for you? If so, why might that be?

Does internalized ableism impact the way you view yourself? What might be the negative consequences of this?

SECTION 3

WHAT IS DBT AND HOW CAN IT HELP?

Many of the skills in this book come from dialectical behavior therapy (DBT), a type of therapy developed by psychologist Marsha Linehan to address emotional challenges that make everyday life difficult. Skills are one of the core parts of DBT. These skills give practical steps to help with life's difficulties and achieve a person's goals. DBT clinicians frequently talk about "building a life worth living." Everyone gets to decide for themselves what this looks like. There are four sets of skills that help get us there:

- **MINDFULNESS** skills help us live in the present moment and make choices more effectively. They allow us to take part in life as it is right now.

- **DISTRESS TOLERANCE** skills get us through intense situations without making them worse. Sometimes people cope with difficulties by using drugs or alcohol. They may injure themselves on purpose or explode at other people. These kinds of strategies usually make people feel worse afterward. Distress tolerance skills don't change the situation, but they can get us through it with less chaos.

- **EMOTIONAL REGULATION** skills help us feel our emotions without letting them run our lives. Intense emotions can be enjoyable but can also leave us feeling like we're on a rollercoaster. Increasing regulation lets us have more choice in acting on our emotions. These skills also teach about the importance of emotions. Sometimes emotions feel like so much work—it would be nice to just turn them off! However, emotions give us important information about ourselves and other people.

- **INTERPERSONAL EFFECTIVENESS** skills focus on satisfying relationships with others. This includes setting boundaries with other people. It also means learning how to speak up for your own needs.

WHEN TO SEEK ADDITIONAL HELP

Everyone has emotional struggles from time to time. People with chronic emotional dysregulation might have big mood swings, high anxiety, or angry outbursts. They may have a lot of conflict with other people. They may try to cope with these issues through drugs or alcohol, eating disorders, or other self-harming behaviors. If you have these challenges, you might want to talk to the adults in your life about exploring a DBT program. A lot of research shows DBT is helpful for teens struggling with serious challenges. A full program offers many forms of support for you and your family.

LETTING OPPOSITE THINGS BE TRUE

The "dialectical" part of DBT means bringing together opposites to create a deeper understanding. Instead of holding to one truth, we look to see that seemingly opposite things can be true at one time.

Beth and her boyfriend Quentin frequently fight because they don't spend as much time together as Beth wants. Quentin has been preoccupied with health issues, as well as some recent losses in his family. Though Beth understands this, she becomes very sad when Quentin does not text her back as quickly as she wants or when he has to cancel plans. "It's like he doesn't even care about me." Quentin says his feelings have not changed toward Beth, but he is overwhelmed with life stressors. It hurts when Beth says he clearly doesn't care about her.

Right now, Beth is engaging in black-and-white thinking, where she can only see one side of the argument: Quentin doesn't reach out as much as she wants, so he doesn't care about her. Meanwhile, Quentin insists he does care. They find themselves arguing repeatedly about this point.

A dialectical perspective for this situation might be:

- Beth feels uncared for by Quentin's absence, *and*
- Quentin is going through a lot, which makes showing up for Beth difficult.

Acknowledging both of these truths can help Quentin and Beth get unstuck. Beth may decide that though she cares about Quentin, the relationship is too stressful, and she wants to end it. Or she may decide that, though it is challenging right now, she and Quentin do love each other, so she will stay. They may find ways to connect that better meet both their needs; for example, they might text each other silly memes as a low-key way to connect throughout the day.

LEARNING CHANGE AND ACCEPTANCE

One of the central dialectics in DBT is *change and acceptance*. Remember J from section 2, who denied their sensory sensitivities? Once J accepted their needs, they could make changes to improve their life. They gave themself permission to wear earplugs and take breaks. J could say, "I accept that I have a lot of sensory needs, *and* I can take steps to support my needs." J initially wanted to be different. They only focused on change and had no acceptance of their sensitivities. Yet wishing they were different did not create change. It was only when they accepted themself that change followed.

Other examples of a dialectic include "You are trying hard, *and* you need to try harder to meet your goal of being first clarinet"; "I am a strong and capable person, *and* I need help sometimes"; and "I hate my parents, *and* I love them."

Some neurodivergent brains are especially prone to getting stuck in black-and-white thinking. Being rigidly on one end of a dialectic can make us stuck.

Eliot won first place in the science fair with his working Lego model of Roman aqueducts. He is really excited, as he worked hard. Eliot also feels guilty because his friend also worked hard but didn't place at all. Eliot's family wants to celebrate his win, but he thinks, "It's wrong to celebrate when my friend is disappointed." His brother sees his hesitation and talks to him privately. With his brother's help, Eliot is able to see that he can be both sad for his friend and proud of his project. He plans to text his friend later, and he will go out with his family for dinner to celebrate.

Practicing dialectical thinking can help us see more nuance in situations, understand others' perspectives, and see situations more clearly.

FOR YOU TO DO

Is there anywhere you feel stuck in one perspective? Practice using dialectical thinking to identify the opposite perspective, as well as holding both sides together, and see if any new insights develop.

MY PERSPECTIVE	AN OPPOSITE OR DIFFERENT PERSPECTIVE	DIALECTICAL STATEMENT THAT HOLDS BOTH PERSPECTIVES	NEW INSIGHTS
Eliot: I am excited I won the science fair.	My friend is sad. It's wrong to celebrate when she's sad.	I am excited I won, and I am sad that my friend is disappointed.	Celebrating my win doesn't mean I don't care about my friend. I can feel proud of myself and still offer her support.

SECTION 4
SENSITIVITY

Sensitivity. It's a loaded topic for many of us, often used as a put-down or a way to dismiss feelings. What *is* sensitivity, however? Simply put, *sensitivity* means how responsive you are to input. There are two broad categories this falls into:

- **INTERNAL INPUT:** thoughts, feelings, interpretations, and internal sensory cues such as pain or hunger

- **EXTERNAL INPUT:** smells, lights, temperatures, the emotions of other people

Elaine Aron, the psychologist who first identified the highly sensitive type, estimates that 15 to 20 percent of people are born highly sensitive. Being highly sensitive does not mean you are being dramatic or willfully difficult, just as it does not make you better than other people. It just means you are picking up on more input than the average person does.

Everyone feels more sensitive from time to time. If you are worried about a big project for school, you might be bothered by things you would normally shrug off. If the person you're seeing breaks things off, you might feel highly aware of love songs. Trauma tends to make people sensitive to reminders of the trauma they have experienced. (If this is true for you, therapy can help reduce or eliminate these triggers.) Some people experience higher sensitivity as a baseline, however. If this is you, it is important to understand and accept your sensitivity.

SENSITIVITY IN ACTION

Read through these common experiences of sensitivity and check off those that apply to you:

- [ ] overhead lights feel too bright

- [ ] very aware of other people's moods (even when they don't seem to be aware of their moods!)

- [ ] emotions last a long time

- [ ] slow to transition out of an emotion

- [ ] high emotional highs—and low lows

- [ ] needing to retreat to recenter yourself

- [ ] aware of small changes in the environment

- [ ] eye contact is too intense

- [ ] needing a long time to process emotions and experiences

- [ ] difficulty with "small talk"

- [ ] medicine or substances like caffeine have a strong impact

- [ ] concerned with fairness

- [ ] feeling overwhelmed easily

- [ ] striving for perfection

- ☐ minor criticism can feel incredibly harsh

- ☐ rich inner life

- ☐ dislike of certain textures

- ☐ high sense of empathy toward other humans, animals, and the environment

- ☐ physical sensitivities (skin, digestion, etc.)

- ☐ noticing subtleties others may not notice (e.g., the fan of a computer)

WHO IS SENSITIVE?

If you checked a number of the boxes on the previous list, you are likely highly sensitive. This may surprise you, especially if you are extroverted or have high energy. There are stereotypes about what sensitive people "look like," but sensitivity occurs in all different types of people.

People of all gender, racial, and cultural backgrounds can have high sensitivity. Stereotypes and biases can make it harder for some people to be recognized as sensitive. In the US, women have more freedom to be sensitive than men do. The sensitivity of people of color is often overlooked by white people. It also may not be safe for some people to show their sensitivity. If this is true for you, it is especially important for you to validate your own sensitivity.

Many types of neurodivergence involve increased sensitivity—it's not just limited to self-identified highly sensitive people. Autistic people and ADHDers in particular are often quite sensitive. *Rejection sensitive dysphoria (RSD)* is a specific type of emotional sensitivity that often goes along with ADHD; we will discuss RSD further in section 27.

SENSITIVITY: THE GOOD AND THE BAD

It's easy to identify the challenges of sensitivity, like annoying sensory input. You may be strongly affected by an intense political discussion or scenes of violence. Maybe you just need a lot of time to recover every day.

Sometimes people resent these challenges and try to push past their limits. But when you ignore your own needs, it is easy to crash emotionally and physically. This can lead to a vicious cycle of judging yourself for being so affected, or being judged by other people, and then pushing yourself even harder to "be normal."

> **Ayesha** wants to go to the county fair with her friends but feels overwhelmed by the crowds, the lights, and the noise. Some of the rides are exciting but can be overstimulating. Ayesha judges herself for feeling dread about the fair. Last year, she forced herself to go on all the rides and ended up crying on the way home.

Sensitivity itself is a neutral trait, and it's important to remember there are many benefits of being sensitive. Think of someone who shows a new classmate where the art supplies are because they noticed the new classmate looked lost. Sensory input can be annoying, but it also adds richness to daily life. Birds singing or a fresh cup of coffee may be deeply enjoyable for a sensitive person.

> **Ayesha** decides to go to the fair but waits to get on the rides until she's gotten used to the crowds. She wears earplugs to muffle noise. She and a friend get a snack and listen to a band playing to a small audience. Ayesha enjoys identifying the part each instrument is playing and loses herself in the music as she and her friend dance.

FOR YOU TO DO

Look at the list of sensitive characteristics under "Sensitivity in Action," and reflect on how sensitivity has shown up in your life. **Are there things about yourself that you understand differently now?**

Are there things you like about being sensitive? Things you would change if you could?

SECTION 5
INTENSITY

Many neurodivergent people experience life at a high intensity. Emotions, thoughts, interests, and sensory experiences are stronger than neurotypical people typically experience them as. This could look like:

- persistently debating your own point of view

- moving quickly into strong emotions

- feeling driven to do a lot of research to comprehensively understand a subject—or just for fun!

- going beyond the requirements for a project because you find the subject so interesting

- having very strong likes and dislikes

- feeling a lot of energy, followed by a crash

- fixating on a particular topic or person

- meltdowns or shutdowns when overwhelmed

- strong responses to sensory input

Sometimes this intensity is misunderstood and can be incorrectly diagnosed as a mental health condition. Intensity as a trait is associated with many forms of neurodivergence. It does not necessarily mean someone has a mood disorder.

Often, intensity is judged against what society considers appropriate. In the United States, it's considered normal to be a big fan of an NFL team and wear their gear, follow the stats, and watch every game. Feeling devastated after a team's big loss is acceptable. It's less acceptable to feel devastated over the death of a character in a comic book series or the extinction of an animal species.

> Eliot has an intense interest in the Roman Empire and is creative at fitting it into his assignments. For his government class, he wrote a paper on the influence of Roman architecture on public buildings in the US. In chemistry class, Eliot did a presentation on Roman concrete techniques. When it's Eliot's turn to pick a movie, his family knows it will be a historical epic. Eliot generally has a laid-back attitude—until he starts talking about his favorite Roman military campaigns. His mother compares his "infodumping" to a fire hose.

Much like sensitivity, intensity is a neutral trait. At times, it can be fun and beneficial to feel things so strongly. It can also be distressing if you frequently feel intensely sad or angry.

THE EXPERIENCE OF INTENSITY

At times, people may wish they could tone down their intensity. It can be fun to feel eight hundred thoughts in your brain, but it also makes it more difficult for you to express yourself. Where do you start when eight hundred thoughts are fighting to be first out of your mouth? It might be nice to not feel so much or to just enjoy a book without being very aware of the ableist tropes it reinforces.

Other people may not understand or share your intensity. Family and friends may not want to analyze a situation in as much depth as you'd like. They may feel content to say "that was a good movie" without wanting to discuss the plot, production, how it compares to similar movies, and applying a feminist lens to the story.

Intensity can affect others in ways that are worth considering. If you declare your undying love after a first date, that could feel overwhelming to your date. If you scream at your mom when she asks you to put your dinner plate in the kitchen, it can be frightening.

You may be very aware of how your intensity can impact others or not aware at all. Being intense does not mean that you are a "bad person," but it is helpful to have some ability to moderate your expressions of intensity when it comes to other people.

Eliot's dad is his best audience for his infodumping. His dad has some shared interest in the Roman Empire. When his dad comes home from work, Eliot is often waiting to share something with him. His dad is patient and interested but often tired when he gets home from work. After many discussions, Eliot and his dad have come up with a system. Eliot will give his dad the "headline" when he comes home. After his dad has eaten, he'll ask Eliot to share what he's learned. Eliot wants to share his knowledge as soon as his dad comes home, but he is okay with this system. It's more satisfying to have his dad as an interested audience.

Learning when to turn on and off expressions of intensity is helpful. It can help you meet your own goals or act more effectively. Later, we'll discuss more of what this looks like and how it's different from masking. But you need to have places to express your intensity. This could be with a family member, like Eliot, on a Discord server, or even in your own journal.

FOR YOU TO DO

In what ways does intensity show up in your life?

What do you enjoy about intensity? What is harder for you?

SECTION 6
EFFECTIVENESS

The word "effective" describes doing what works rather than:

- what we wish would work

- what we (or others) think should work

- what we consider fair or "right"

Beliefs and emotions can prevent us from taking the actions needed to improve a situation. Ableism is one belief that can block effective action. Another thing that can block effectiveness is having a habit of or an attachment to doing things in a particular way.

> Jules has always waited until the night before an assignment is due to write her papers. She rarely studies for exams and relies on her memory for tests. For the first two years of high school, Jules could do this and still make the honor roll. In her junior year, however, she started taking harder classes and working part time. Just listening to the lecture without studying and writing papers at the last minute no longer works, given the increased workload and demands on her time. She is constantly stressed and falling behind. However, Jules believes that "I'm smart, and I should be able to do this."

Jules is acting ineffectively here by not accepting that she is no longer able to stay on top of her schoolwork using her old strategies while still making the same grades.

Sometimes the environment prevents us from being effective. One of the hard things about being a teenager is that a lot of decisions are out of your control. Adults in your life can help you access services and supports—or deny them. Teachers and schools may be more or less supportive of accommodations, even if you have a 504 plan or Individualized Education Program (IEP).

Twelve-year-old **Yichen** was assessed as an ADHDer after his school noted the gap between his abilities and his grades. Yichen was relieved to have this explanation instead of just thinking, "There's something wrong with me." The psychologist who did the assessment recommended some accommodations that Yichen's family could ask for at school and mentioned the potential of medication. Yichen is interested in these possibilities. However, Yichen's mother rejected the psychologist's finding and recommendations, as she believes Yichen simply has a willpower problem. Yichen is frustrated by this. He has tried to implement some strategies from a book for ADHD kids. Though he still struggles in school, he doesn't see himself as a failure. Yichen plans to pursue other supports when he is eighteen.

To act more effectively, we need to let go of judgments of how things "should" be. For people driven by a high sense of ethics, as many neurodivergent people are, this can be challenging. You may get stuck on the idea that one specific way is right—or wrong. Sometimes, determining what you want to accomplish and focusing on that can make it easier to identify effective action. If you want to make friends, but don't talk to anyone in person or online, it will be very difficult to make friends!

Ayesha joined the youth symphony to meet other people who are as serious about music as she is. She feels shy and avoids talking to new people. She hides in the bathroom until just before practice starts and then rushes to her seat. At the end of practice, she runs out to the parking lot. Ayesha realizes this makes it hard to get to know anyone, so she asks her cousin for advice. With his help, she decides to try talking to a flute player who always wears a hoodie from a local animal shelter. Ayesha compliments her hoodie and shares her own love for animals. When another clarinet player invites their section for extra practice, Ayesha goes even though she feels nervous.

Being effective is not always easy. Many of the skills in this workbook will help you be more effective.

FOR YOU TO DO

What is an area of your life where things are not working as you would like them to?

_____

_____

_____

_____

What are your blocks to being effective? These can be internal or external.

_____

_____

_____

_____

_____

_____

What skills, tools, or supports do you need to be more effective?

_____

_____

_____

_____

_____

_____

SECTION 7
COGNITIVE FLEXIBILITY

Cognitive flexibility refers to your brain's capacity to change and adapt to new information. It's helpful in a number of ways, because it helps you:

- **UNDERSTAND DIFFERENT PERSPECTIVES.** A committed carnivore might be able to hear and understand their vegan friend's arguments for only eating plants, even if they don't decide to become vegan too.

- **CHANGE YOUR THOUGHTS AS NEW INFORMATION COMES IN.** You might find a new board game boring and seemingly random. As the game progresses, though, you may start to understand how it works and learn that you really enjoy it.

- **THINK ABOUT MULTIPLE THINGS AT THE SAME TIME.** Your English teacher might ask you to read a book and be aware of both the plot and symbolism.

- **CHANGE YOUR BEHAVIOR FOR DIFFERENT ENVIRONMENTS.** Goofing off with friends in the hallway between classes is fine, but teachers expect you to focus on the lesson when in class.

- **EMPATHIZE WITH OTHERS.** Say your friend is upset that she didn't get cast in the school play—but you don't feel the same way about the idea of being in a play yourself. However, your friend probably won't be comforted if you say, "Oh good, being on stage in front of the school sounds awful." Taking your friend's perspective can help you understand how to support her.

- **RESPOND TO CHALLENGES IN THE MOMENT.** Bus lines change, stores stop carrying certain brands, and movies sell out. Being able to adapt to things as they happen can help you deal with problems instead of getting stuck.

- **CREATIVELY SOLVE PROBLEMS.** It's easier to generate solutions when you aren't fixed on one "right way" to handle things.

There are a number of neurodivergences that tend to go along with increased rigidity. Autistic folks and people with anxiety disorders are often less flexible. Many neurodivergent people are comforted by routines and sameness. Being more rigid or fixed is not inherently "bad." It can be great to have strong views that are unshakable! Neurodivergent climate activist Greta Thunberg's steadfast moral authority has impacted the world and inspired thousands to take action on climate change. Someone who is more flexible might not have the same moral clarity as Greta.

At the same time, life often throws us curveballs. It is useful to have cognitive flexibility to navigate these challenges more smoothly. Cognitive flexibility is associated with increased resilience to stress and negative events. If we need things around us to be "just so" to be okay, we are more vulnerable when things are different than we hope.

WHY BE FLEXIBLE?

Rigid thinking can lead to suffering and problems in relationships. If you believe that being friends means you hang out every day, and not hanging out means the friendship is over, it could cause problems when your friends disagree about that. It's important to take in new information and adapt to it.

Sometimes reality doesn't bend to our will. Changes and unexpected events are a regular part of life, even if we don't enjoy them. If we are too rigid, it can block us from effectively responding to change.

When to Be Flexible

- **WHEN YOU HAVE TO BE.** Your favorite teacher is out sick, and you have a substitute.

- **WHEN BEING FLEXIBLE IS MORE IN ALIGNMENT WITH YOUR GOALS.** If you really want to be involved with the school play, you might accept a part that is different from the one you were hoping for.

- **WHEN BEING FLEXIBLE ALIGNS WITH YOUR VALUES.** You and your mom take turns picking which place to order pizza from. She likes a place that you think is just okay. Since fairness is really important to you, you put up with her pizza choice, because your mom does the same for you.

There are also times when it's better to *not* be flexible. We'll discuss this more later in the section on boundaries, but here are a few times when you might choose to not be flexible:

- when something violates your values

- when you feel that you're already compromising a lot

- when being flexible would hurt you

How to Be Flexible

The next part of this book is focused on mindfulness, which helps increase cognitive flexibility. Mindfulness also helps you develop the ability to view your internal experience more objectively. This can be helpful for recognizing when you are cognitively stuck.

Even simply knowing that you tend to be inflexible is helpful. You can use that knowledge to prompt yourself: "Is there another way to look at this?" You can also plan to give yourself time to mentally shift gears if needed.

Practice taking different perspectives to increase cognitive flexibility. Art is especially helpful for this. If you have a favorite TV show or book, you could try to think through how different characters would respond to a situation. You could also challenge yourself to come up with different interpretations for events.

If you tend to be less cognitively flexible, it will take time and a lot of energy to practice flexibility. Sometimes, being deliberately inflexible in one area can free up energy to be flexible elsewhere. Apple founder Steve Jobs created a uniform to wear every day. Not having to decide what to wear left him with more mental energy to be creative at work. Having a routine for yourself or eating the same breakfast every day can give you more ability to be flexible where you want to be.

Eliot has been planning for his dream Roman vacation. He is nervous, as travel will require a lot of flexibility from him. To increase his flexibility, he signs up for the debate club. The club sponsor assigns debate positions to the students. Even if the students personally disagree with the position they're assigned, they have to argue for it. Eliot also gets a book of lateral thinking games. These puzzles require "out of the box" thinking. Though they felt impossible at first, with practice, they are getting easier for Eliot.

FOR YOU TO DO

Is cognitive flexibility something you struggle with? How does it show up for you?

Where would you like to be more flexible?

Are there routines that you can establish to free up more mental space to be flexible when needed?

SECTION 8
EXECUTIVE FUNCTIONING

Executive functioning consists of a set of mental skills that help with daily life tasks. These skills help us plan for the future, meet our goals, and avoid problems. They include:

ORGANIZING	To accomplish tasks, we usually need to organize our thoughts. This could look like figuring out the structure of an essay or figuring out each role in a group project. We also have to organize physical environments. It's hard to do your homework if it's buried under a stack of other papers or to get dressed if all your clothes are piled on the floor.
STAYING FOCUSED	Not getting distracted easily is a skill, whether you're tuning out thoughts about your crush or the noise of the air conditioner. Being able to focus means being able to ignore these distractions— or returning to focus after you've been distracted. Sometimes, you do have to make adjustments to meet sensory needs, or something surprising happens that naturally grabs your attention. Being able to return to what you were doing is an important executive functioning skill.
REMEMBERING DETAILS	Where's your bus pass? When's your best friend's birthday? When are your library books due? These are often small things that have a big impact on your life. People usually appreciate it if you remember information about them, and forgetting it can hurt relationships. Losing items can cost time and money.

WORKING MEMORY	Working memory refers to temporary storage for information you need to act on now. Working memory is what helps you remember the name of someone you just met or the bathroom code the cashier just gave you. If your working memory is poor, you may end up with a lot of incomplete tasks. You might start to take out the trash, then notice that the dog's water bowl is empty. If you stop to fill the water bowl, you might forget that you were gathering the trash. If you continue taking out the trash, you might forget about the water bowl by the time you're done with the trash.
FLEXIBILITY	The ability to change your thoughts when presented with new information and events. If you plan to go on a walk and a thunderstorm starts, you need to change plans. Mental flexibility also helps with taking different perspectives. (It doesn't mean you have to agree with those perspectives!)
SELF-CONTROL	The ability to resist blurting out thoughts or to resist acting impulsively on emotions. Self-control also helps make decisions in line with your values, needs, and goals. You might want to play video games all night, but if you also want to get up early to watch a soccer game, self-control will get you to bed early.
PRIORITIZING TASKS	Identifying what is most urgent. It's helpful to know which assignment is most important to do first—maybe the one that is due first, the one worth the most points, or the one in a class where you're on the verge of failing. Without being able to prioritize tasks, it can feel hard to know where to start.

ORDERING A SEQUENCE	Determining the order of steps to take in a task. This often requires being able to visualize the whole process. For example, when cooking a pasta dish, you often begin with boiling the water, even when you want the pasta to be the last thing to finish cooking. That's because it takes water a while to boil. To make dinner quickly and efficiently, you need to order the tasks: boil water, work on sauce, cook pasta.
TIME MANAGEMENT	Estimating how much time a task will take, and factoring in what else needs doing. If you know it takes you a while to do your Spanish homework, you know you can't wait to do it in homeroom, ten minutes before your Spanish class. (However, if you're very quick at your Spanish homework, you could plan to do it then!) Being able to take a look at what else is on your plate is helpful as well. If you have a paper due next week, and you also have a lot of babysitting jobs next week, you might start to work on your paper this weekend. Challenges with time management can cause a lot of stress.
BREAKING DOWN STEPS	You might have an idea of what you want to do, but not be sure how to make it a reality. It's one thing to visualize a cool cosplay costume you could make, but actually making it could involve researching, creating sketches, getting a pattern or fabric, ironing the fabric, and then finally sewing the costume. If you can't identify the steps, that can make it difficult to create the costume or plan how much time you will need.
TASK INITIATION	Taking the first step on something you have to do, whether it's starting a school project or designing a Dungeons and Dragons campaign. Getting started can be the hardest part!

Often these skills are interlocking. If you can break down the steps of a task, it's easier to estimate how long it will take. Having stronger self-control skills can help you return to focusing after a distraction. If you take a break from homework to look up basketball trade news, self-control lets you move back to your homework, instead of doing a deep dive on videos about the top trade prospects.

No one is born with these executive functioning skills! They develop over time, with experience and brain development. Like any skill, some people seem to pick them up with little coaching or even intuitively. How strong your executive functioning skills are has nothing to do with your intelligence or your character.

It's also worth noting that many of these skills—or struggles with them—become challenges only in certain environments! Being in school with many deadlines and multiple classes is more taxing than taking one class during summer school. And taking one class during summer school is more demanding still than being home sick, where you can just lay on the couch and watch funny YouTube videos. Culture also plays a part: in cultures that are more flexible with time, there's less pressure.

While no one has perfect executive functioning at all times, it can be especially challenging for neurodivergent folks. ADHDers may struggle with focusing, task initiation, and breaking tasks down into steps. Depression can also make it harder to focus and impact working memory. Bipolar disorder can lead to impulsive actions. Trauma can make self-control difficult, as strong emotions take over or urges to escape lead to risky behavior. Demand avoidance can also look like executive functioning issues (we'll talk about this later). Many autistic people get more rigid under stress—and in fact, stress itself makes executive functioning more challenging.

You may have challenges in some or all of these areas. It's important to recognize them as challenges with executive functioning—not as character defects. Others may see executive functioning challenges as signs that you're lazy or don't care. You might think that yourself. It can be frustrating to hear "Why can't you just...?" But executive functioning challenges aren't just willfulness, and it's harder to make changes and access supports if you think it's "just how I am."

Many kids rely on the adults around them to help support executive functioning. As you get older, this becomes more of your responsibility. While getting support from others is helpful, that support may not always be accessible. It can also feel empowering to explore what works best for you. You may not be the best at these tasks, but you can still improve and meet your goals.

Drew is a gifted fifteen-year-old. They are able to do college-level math easily, but keeping track of their keys is another story. Drew's family jokes about them being the "absent-minded professor," but no one is laughing when Drew holds up the family most mornings because they can't find their backpack. Drew is also trying to save up money for a big Lego set that they're excited about. They're having a hard time saving, however, because after a Saturday mowing lawns, they head to the arcade and spend most of what they've earned. Drew feels frustrated because "I'm too smart to struggle with this stuff."

WHAT HELPS WITH EXECUTIVE FUNCTIONING?

Your executive functioning abilities are not set in stone. There are many factors and strategies that support executive functioning tasks. Let's look at a few:

- **MATURITY.** As a teen, your brain is still going through significant development. As your brain matures, executive functioning tends to improve.

- **MEDICATION AND THERAPY.** Medication can help if ADHD is at play. Treating an underlying mood disorder can also help if that's the cause of your difficulties. Similarly, if trauma is a factor, getting treatment for trauma is important and will improve your life overall.

- **SELF-ACCEPTANCE.** Remind yourself that you have executive functioning challenges—that you're not lazy or uncaring. You can create more supports for yourself, but it will take a while. It's so important to have patience with yourself.

- **ACCOMMODATIONS.** If you have a diagnosis that qualifies for supports at school, you can make requests in your 504 plan or IEP. Even if you don't have a formal plan, you can ask for help from teachers or the school tutoring center.

- **EXECUTIVE SUPPORTS.** Clocks, timers, and alarms are your friends! To develop time-estimating skills, guess how long it will take to do the dishes. Note the time when you start, and check when you're done with the task. How close was your guess? You can also use a paper or electronic calendar to set reminders for regular events, such as family birthdays. If you want to take a half hour break when you're done with school and then start homework, you can set an alarm where your textbooks are. When the half hour is up, you'll have to go over to the textbooks to turn it off.

- **BUILD IN "STOPS."** Make it more difficult to engage in impulsive action. If you're going shopping, only take a small amount of cash. Or put a note on your wallet to remind you of a goal you're working toward—getting a guitar, for example—to give you a pause before buying something that catches your eye. Put blocks on certain apps on your phone or websites on your computer to prevent yourself from endlessly scrolling social media. Having to manually enter passwords (instead of saving them) can help too.

- **WORK BACKWARD.** Visualize what you want your end result to be. If you imagine having friends over to watch a movie and eat snacks, you have some clues as to what needs to happen first: ask friends, pick out a movie, and get snacks. If you're not sure what else you would need to do, you can run your plan by someone and see if there's anything you've missed, such as checking to make sure you don't already have plans that day.

- **TAKE THE FIRST STEP.** If you need to make flashcards for a vocabulary list, you might get out the paper to make the cards (or download an app). Sometimes, just taking the initial step will get you going further. Even if that initial step is all you do, you've at least started on your task—and made it so you have one less thing to do later.

- **EXPERIMENT.** What works for your friend might not work for you. In fact, many standard solutions may not work for neurodivergent people. For example, a common tip for getting organized is to aim for a minimalist look, where you hide as much as you can out of sight. However, for many ADHDers, out of sight is out of mind. Having things in clear view helps keep them from disappearing from your mind.

- **MAKE IT FUN.** Many neurodivergent people have what is sometimes called "an interest-based nervous system." This means that if you find something interesting or even fun, it is dramatically easier to do. How can you use your interests to make tasks a game? You might like racing against a timer to see how many dishes you can find in your room in fifteen minutes. Or you could pretend that instead of just doing geography homework, you are a spy learning the territory of a mission.

- **REFLECT.** Look at what things you have tried from this list and how well they went. The goal here is to improve your skills, not to shame yourself! If you were trying to practice better time management, did you estimate enough time for the task? Perhaps you realized you forgot to factor in the library's open hours when you planned your study time. Or maybe you overestimated how long something would take you, and now you know that you can read books for literature class pretty quickly.

Drew picks a spot near the front door where they will put their essential school gear. They make a sign on bright yellow paper that stands out a lot and reads "Keys, Backpack, Library Books." They also set an alarm on their phone to go off each night to remind themself to put their things by the door, and a backup alarm too. This has made the mornings smoother. Drew's dad has made a game where the first kid in the car, with all their stuff, gets to pick the music. Drew has also reflected on their goal of buying the Lego set and realized it's not realistic to think that they won't spend any money at all. They are experimenting with bringing only a small amount of money to the arcade after mowing. They've accepted that this will mean it takes longer to get the set. Drew's parents remind them that everyone has things that are easy and hard.

FOR YOU TO DO

Do you have challenges with any of the executive functions listed in this section? Which ones are most challenging for you? Are there any areas where your executive functioning is very strong?

How can these strategies reduce the impact of executive functioning challenges? Choose two strategies and write a plan to implement them.

SECTION 9
DEMAND AVOIDANCE

Demand avoidance is the urge to resist performing expected behavior. While we often think of a demand as being hostile or overt, such as a demanding coach who yells and expects perfection, demands come in many forms. They can be:

- **INTERNAL,** such as biological needs like hunger or tiredness. Your own hopes, plans, or goals can also feel like a demand.

- **EXTERNAL,** like rules set by your family or school, homework, a dress code, or laws and regulations.

- **EXPLICIT** expectations, such as homework or chores assigned to you.

- **IMPLICIT,** or unspoken expectations, like norms around making eye contact or limiting how long you talk about a subject that really interests you.

Demands can overlap as well. Physical hunger is an internal demand, and your scheduled lunch break at work is an external demand—and the combined pressure of both can be very challenging.

Almost anything can feel like a demand. In fact, the exercises in this workbook could be a demand! Demand avoidance is a common experience for neurodivergent people. In fact, everyone—neurodivergent or neurotypical—experiences demand avoidance at times. The difference is in how intense and frequent the demand avoidance is. Demand avoidance can look like outright refusal. It can also involve creative or indirect ways of getting out of tasks, such as pretending you don't see the relative who is clearly expecting a hug. Being the class clown can also be a demand avoidance strategy. If your teacher calls on you and you make a joke out of it, you might be able to get away with not answering the question!

42

What sort of things typically trigger demand avoidance?

- sensory overstimulation or understimulation

- changes in routine

- transitioning from one activity to another

- not understanding why something is expected

- the pressure of expectation—from yourself or others

- the expectation to do something that isn't interesting to you

- feeling maxed out from already having high levels of stress

- uncertainty about how to do a task

It's usual for demand avoidance to fluctuate. Sometimes you can do something fairly easily and then on another day, it will be much harder or even impossible. Parents, teachers, or you yourself might think this is a sign you are being "willful." But demand avoidance doesn't feel like a choice when you're experiencing it. It feels like overwhelming anxiety.

Aaliyah is an autistic fifteen-year-old who was referred to a DBT program after her family learned she had been self-harming. Aaliyah wants to stop her self-harm and is interested in the DBT program. However, she feels overwhelmed by the skills group homework. Even tracking her self-harm urges on a daily basis is hard to do most days. Aaliyah feels stressed and thinks her group leader doesn't like her. Her individual therapist spent last session trying to get Aaliyah to commit to doing the homework.

A NOTE ON PATHOLOGICAL DEMAND AVOIDANCE

Pathological demand avoidance (sometimes renamed "persistent" or "pervasive drive for autonomy") is a suggested profile of autism that is involves high levels of demand avoidance, to the point that it becomes a substantial issue in one's life. PDA is recognized in some countries, such as the UK, but not officially recognized in the US. There are arguments about whether PDA is a separate profile of autism or a misdiagnosis of anxiety or trauma. Yet it is a profile that many people relate to and strongly identify with.

Experiencing demand avoidance does not inherently mean you are a PDAer. PDAers report feeling such intense demand avoidance that even doing things they want to do is difficult or impossible. If you're a PDAer, your grandmother making your favorite meal could feel like a demand. If you relate to these statements, then it might be worth looking into PDA. There is also more to PDA than just demand avoidance. For example, PDAers often present as highly social and can be incredibly creative in the strategies they use to cope with demands.

HOW TO COPE WITH DEMAND AVOIDANCE

First, simply knowing that it's demand avoidance that you're dealing with can be helpful in reducing self-blame and stories around "just being difficult." Next, evaluate if you need or want to meet the demands imposed on you. If the demand is optional, drop it. Mindfully choose to put off homework for a day. Wash your hair tomorrow instead.

If a demand can't be avoided entirely, see if you can modify it to be more accessible. This could look like eating a granola bar instead of a "proper meal" or observing a class discussion instead of participating. Save your energy for demands you must meet.

Sometimes there are demands that need to be met as they are, or there will be serious consequences. If you need to take medication, there might not be much room for modifying that. You might live in a highly structured environment like a shelter, where you have to follow the rules. Using language that frames things as a choice can help remind you why you're doing something. "I'm choosing to attend school because I like the cafeteria's cinnamon rolls and want to see my friends." "I'm choosing to take insulin because I don't want to go to the hospital again."

Requests made with indirect language can also ease the stress of demands. Indirect language often involves statements of fact rather than simple requests. Someone saying, "It's time to eat," puts some pressure on you to eat, right now. "There's enchiladas on the stove" is just some information about food that is available. There is not an explicit expectation to eat the enchiladas, now or at any time. This strategy can "get around" demand avoidance and make eating easier.

Reminding yourself of your values, and acting from them, can also help with demands. If you look at attending your cousin's wedding as a demand, it might be harder for you to go than if you look at it as living out your value of showing up for family.

Being playful can also reduce the impact of demands. Games like racing your best friend to see who can complete the math worksheet first can be motivating. Engaging in pretend play is another way to make tasks more fun. You're not a socially anxious person at a party, you're an anthropologist observing the birthday customs of this culture! PE class might feel more bearable if you imagine you're the barbarian warrior you play in Dungeons and Dragons, and you're training to go fight a giant.

"Vacations" from demands, as much as possible, are also helpful for resetting. While we can't ever fully avoid all demands—we still need to eat and rest—finding time that minimizes the demands placed on you is helpful. This could be a few hours on a weekend morning or spending your lunch hour in the library where it's quiet and you don't have to interact with anyone.

Aaliyah emailed her therapists an article about demand avoidance. She spoke one-on-one with her therapist and group leader about how she wants to do DBT but demand avoidance sometimes makes it hard to do homework. Her therapist did a values exercise with Aaliyah to help her see how becoming more skillful will align with her core values. Now at the end of sessions, her therapist states, "There's a stack of diary cards by the door," instead of saying, "Don't forget to pick up a diary card!" Aaliyah's group leader is still working with her to help make the homework more doable. They're currently experimenting with more clearly explaining how each skill fits in the bigger picture of Aaliyah's goals. Aaliyah sometimes motivates herself by imagining she needs to learn the skills to teach them as a psychologist herself one day. They haven't figured out the best strategy yet, but Aaliyah feels more comfortable in group knowing that her leader understands that she isn't being willfully difficult.

If demand avoidance is causing a lot of stress in your life, bigger changes may be a good idea. Many teens who find the sensory and social aspects of school overwhelming switch to online school, for example. If demand avoidance is causing significant challenges on an ongoing basis, it's important to talk to the adults in your life about it. Understanding that demand avoidance is not willful behavior is important information for them to have.

FOR YOU TO DO

When do you experience demand avoidance? Identify three situations where it tends to come up.

Check off which strategies seem like they could help you with demand avoidance:

☐ Skipping demands

☐ Modifying demands

☐ Connecting to values

☐ Looking at something as a choice rather than a demand

☐ Reframing things in indirect language

☐ Making things into a game

☐ Taking a vacation

How could you use one of these strategies to help with demand avoidance?

_____

_____

_____

_____

_____

_____

_____

PART 2

TAKING CARE OF YOURSELF

SECTION 10
SELF-VALIDATION

Validation is how we show that we're trying to understand someone's thoughts, feelings, and experiences. Listening to someone's experience without judging or trying to change it is a powerful way to be supportive. When we feel validated, we feel better understood. It feels good to have someone say what we're thinking or feeling makes sense. Validation helps us feel safer.

It's important for us all to feel validated, both by other people and ourselves. (We'll discuss how to validate others in section 32.) Sometimes, self-validation is all we have. It's certainly what we have the most control over. If you constantly tell yourself how stupid you are, it's likely to increase painful emotions like shame. If you invalidate your own sensory needs, it's harder to meet them—but it doesn't make those sensory needs go away! Validation can also help with solving problems. If you can validate your emotions and needs, you can take action on them.

When we are chronically invalidated, including by ourselves, it can lead to:

- shame and emotional pain

- judgment toward ourselves and others

- self-criticism, even self-hatred

- thought loops where one moment of invalidation makes us start recounting all the other times we were invalidated

- thoughts that there is something bad or wrong with us at our core

- doubting our own experiences

- difficulty trusting ourselves

Ongoing invalidation is a factor in developing serious challenges with emotional regulation. Everyone experiences invalidation, but neurodivergent people encounter it constantly. Here are some ways that invalidation may show up:

- **DIRECTLY STATED.** Your doctor may dismiss the pain from a shot as "no big deal," while it's very painful for you. People who need to move their bodies a lot may be constantly criticized in formal settings.

- **ASSUMPTIONS THAT DON'T APPLY TO YOU.** A teacher may give general directions to the class, and everyone else seems to just get what is expected. Meanwhile, you're left wondering how to start. Even if your teacher and classmates are kind, you still might judge yourself for seeming to be the only person who doesn't understand the unspoken assumptions.

- **EXPECTATIONS AND NORMS.** History class is full of difficult topics such as war, colonization, and slavery. Students are expected to have discussions on a purely intellectual level. Showing that you are deeply emotionally moved is outside the norms of classrooms. If you start crying or expressing anger, you might be sent outside of class. But for someone who feels very deeply, or who has a high sense of justice, it can feel inhumane to calmly discuss atrocities.

- **MISUNDERSTANDINGS.** People who find eye contact difficult may be perceived as rude. Someone who focuses by doodling or fidgeting may be judged as not paying attention. Parents might think that an ADHDer's disorganization is "on purpose."

- **SELF-INVALIDATION.** Whether you have long understood your neurodivergence or are just exploring it, you are likely aware of ways you are different from other people. Often, people judge their own differences negatively. If you still enjoy playing with action figures in high school, you might judge yourself because most of your peers don't play with action figures in the same way.

VALIDATION: HOW TO

Self-validation starts by acknowledging your feelings and thoughts as they are happening. Practice using nonjudgmental language. Instead of saying, "I am really screwing up again," you might say, "Chemistry class is really hard for me."

Speaking kindly to yourself is important. Imagine what you would say to a friend in the same situation. Chances are you would be gentler with them. You can also imagine what someone you trust would say to you or even a fictional character.

Remind yourself that your thoughts and feelings make sense given what is happening. Sometimes people shame themselves for having a hard time. This can lead to an unhelpful loop of feeling bad, judging that, and then feeling worse for feeling bad. You might think that whatever invalidation you have experienced isn't a big deal, but if it is hurtful, that is important. Mindfulness skills are also helpful for validating your thoughts and feelings without saying they are objectively true.

Remind yourself of your strengths and the efforts you make. It can be hard to recognize the things that we *are* doing because there is a gap between our ideas and our abilities or skills. Or you might not recognize when you are working hard. If you are trying to focus in class without your stimulant medication, you cannot judge yourself by comparing yourself to a non-ADHDer.

It can be helpful to say affirmative statements to yourself. Here are a few examples:

- My sensory needs are valid even if no one else shares them.
- Everyone makes mistakes.
- It's okay to just do an okay job.
- No one is good at everything.
- I'm coping with a lot.
- My feelings are valid.

FOR YOU TO DO

How do you invalidate yourself?

Imagine a kind, trustworthy person. What would they say about the things you invalidate yourself for?

Create a few statements to help with self-validation.

SECTION 11
IDENTIFYING YOUR VALUES

DBT aims to help people "build a life worth living." That is, a life that brings you personal satisfaction. Each person has their own idea about what makes their life feel worth living. Often, one of those things is living in accordance with your values. Values are the principles that guide your daily priorities and decisions. They're more abstract, broader ideals rather than specific rules.

Neurodivergent people are often very values driven, so it's especially important for you to know what your values are. In fact, it might be difficult to do something unless it connects to your values. For example, you may not prioritize following a rule just because it's a rule but be okay with following if it has meaning for you. An example of this might be stoplights. You might think that it's not the law that makes stopping at red lights the right thing to do but the fact that everyone following traffic lights keeps people safe. (On the other hand, some neurodivergent people value order for its own sake!)

KNOWING WHAT YOU VALUE

It can be helpful to identify values in different areas of your life. You can have different values in different aspects of your life. Someone who enjoys a creative, high-risk job may want a very calm and routine personal life, for example.

Here is a short list of some values and life priorities. Go through this list of values and mark the ones that are important to you with a check mark. Note that your interpretation of these values may differ. There are also plenty of values that aren't on this list. Feel free to make your own edits!

- [ ] **ACHIEVEMENT OR ADVANCEMENT:** gaining status and recognition, achieving big goals

- [ ] **ADVENTURE:** stepping out of the ordinary, engaging with the unknown

- [ ] **COOPERATION:** being part of a larger group, working together

- [ ] **COMPASSION:** offering kindness and concern to others, being led by your heart

- [ ] **CREATIVITY:** using your imagination, expressing originality

- [ ] **DEPENDABILITY:** being trustworthy and solid

- [ ] **FAMILY:** building and contributing to a close family, whether family by blood or choice

- [ ] **FUN:** focusing on what is enjoyable, humorous, lighthearted

- [ ] **GROWTH:** continuing to grow and change throughout life

- [ ] **HARD WORK:** persevering, sticking with a difficult task and seeing it through

- [ ] **HELPING OTHERS:** being of service

- [ ] **INTEGRITY:** living according to your values, following your own inner compass

- [ ] **JUSTICE:** working toward fairness and equality

- [ ] **LEADERSHIP:** being a leader and influencing others

- [ ] **LEARNING:** continually learning new information and changing perspective

- [ ] **PASSION:** deep, emotionally driven interests and goals

- [ ] **SECURITY AND SAFETY:** stability, having your needs met, being out of danger

- [ ] **SPIRITUALITY:** connection with something bigger than yourself, whether in a formal religion or not

- [ ] **STABILITY:** predictability and routine

- [ ] _____

- [ ] _____

- [ ] _____

You may look at this list and think they all sound good. Or maybe it depends on the situation. Sometimes, values can come into conflict. Adventure and safety are often posed as opposites, for example. However, you can follow both values by researching thoroughly before going on a road trip or planning to travel in places where you know someone instead of going off all on your own. Other times, values cannot be reconciled as easily. If you value community and truth, you may be torn between calling out problems in the community on one hand and ignoring what you see to preserve the group on the other. Knowing your highest values can help guide your decisions.

At other times, the risk of a situation will determine your actions. You may most strongly value standing by promises, but if your friend swears you to secrecy about their suicidal thoughts, their safety needs to override values. The risk of your friend acting on their suicidal thoughts is too great.

J has recently been interested in playing with their gender expression, but they feel a bit nervous. They value harmonious relationships and know that some people in their life will likely struggle with seeing J show up with eyeliner or wild, patterned tights. At the same time, J also strongly values authenticity and creativity. J engages in mindfulness practice and connects to their wise mind (more on wise mind in section 17). Through this, J realizes that publicly playing with gender also supports their passion for justice, in that they hope their self-expression will normalize gender creativity. Though J doesn't want to upset anyone they know, experimenting with gender is more in alignment with their values.

As a teenager, you are likely hearing a lot about how you should think about your future. Those choices are often impacted by external factors such as citizenship status or access to money, but even within those limits, different people make different decisions based on their values.

Josie and Angel are best friends. They both come from families where money is hard to come by. Josie is hoping for more stability in her life and to work at a job she finds meaningful. She's worked in childcare the last few years and is thinking about becoming an elementary school teacher. She's been talking with the school counselor about scholarships she can apply for. Angel, on the other hand, doesn't want stability—she wants adventure. Angel feels her upbringing has prepared her "to deal with anything." She's interested in herbal medicine, which connects to her love of ecology and harmony with nature. She also likes that there's a lot to learn about herbs, from the history and folklore to growing and using them medicinally. Angel has been considering traveling around the country to do workstays on different herbal farms.

Living according to your values tends to bring a sense of personal satisfaction. It is not always easy to live up to your values but striving to do so will help you experience your life as worth living.

FOR YOU TO DO

Review the checklist of values above to determine the five or so values that are most important to you and circle them. You can get creative and continue to narrow down your values—for example:

- Use a heart to identify your top values in close relationships.

- Use an asterisk to identify your top values when it comes to school and work.

- Use a star to identify your top values for your personal life.

What values do you hold that are not on the list in this section? How do they show up in your life?

SECTION 12

REDUCING VULNERABILITY FACTORS

Though our culture sometimes acts as if our bodies are just vehicles for our brains, physical and mental health are closely related. Getting enough sleep, eating regularly, taking supplements and medications as prescribed, and engaging in physical exercise are all important for good mental health. These aspects of health are sometimes called vulnerability factors because if they are off balance, we are more vulnerable to intense emotions, poor decision-making, and impulsive behavior. Vulnerability factors can be temporary, such as a day where you do not eat much, or they can be ongoing, such as bipolar disorder or chronic pain.

Neurodivergent people are especially sensitive to the impacts of these vulnerability factors. When emotions tend to be quick and intense, it's easier for low blood sugar to push someone into a dysregulated state. Interoception can make it difficult to identify hunger cues, so you might not recognize you are hungry until you suddenly realize you are painfully hungry. Part of caring for yourself is being aware of these vulnerability factors and trying to plan ahead to reduce their impact.

Juan likes to stay up late and talk with his friends online. When he stays up late, he oversleeps and does not have time to eat breakfast. After tracking his moods, Juan notices that on those days, he gets frustrated easily and is more likely to have a panic attack. Juan decides to get offline early enough to get six hours of sleep, which is a good amount for his body. He also grabs nutritious snacks that he can eat on his way to school if he oversleeps.

Imani has been without her Adderall for a week due to a national shortage of medication. She's feeling stressed about falling behind on schoolwork. Last night, she had a hard time sleeping. When her girlfriend asks to plan their couple's Halloween costume, Imani knows that the discussion would be challenging even under the best of circumstances due to her own perfectionism. Given the other vulnerability factors Imani is experiencing, she asks her girlfriend if they can have that discussion once she has resumed taking Adderall and is caught up on school.

FOR YOU TO DO

Identify your vulnerability factors in the following chart. In the "Where I'm At Now" column, describe what your life looks like currently: how much sleep you get, if you use substances, and so on. In "Where I'd Like to Be," describe your goals in this area. For example, if you currently go to bed at 1 a.m. and get four hours of sleep but would like to work toward an 11 p.m. bedtime, put that in "Where I'd Like to Be."

If you find yourself harshly judging yourself, skip ahead to section 19, Observe and Describe, for help in doing this activity nonjudgmentally.

	WHERE I'M AT NOW	WHERE I'D LIKE TO BE
SLEEP		
EATING		

61

HYDRATION		
MEDICATION		
SUBSTANCES (CAFFEINE, NICOTINE, ETC.)		
HEALTH		
EXERCISE		

Identify one step you can take to reduce your vulnerability factors.

SECTION 13

REFILLING YOUR TANK

Y ou can think of reducing vulnerability factors as a way to help yourself be at a more stable baseline, emotionally and physically. But what about the things that bring you joy? These are important as well. If you think of vulnerability factors and stressors as the things that are withdrawals from your account, then what are you putting into your account?

Check off what nourishes you, and if there's anything you enjoy that's not on this list, write it in on the blank lines at the bottom:

- [ ] spiritual practices

- [ ] time in nature

- [ ] creating art

- [ ] stretching

- [ ] special interests (see section 15)

- [ ] reading

- [ ] researching one of your interests

- [ ] time with friends

- [ ] time with family

- [ ] building with Legos

- [ ] parallel play (where you and another person are together but doing separate activities, such as knitting and listening to a podcast while your best friend reads a book)

- [ ] games

- [ ] sending memes

- [ ] eating a favorite snack

- [ ] listening to or playing music

- [ ] board games

- [ ] creating a new character for a role-playing game

- [ ] wearing an outfit you carefully planned

- [ ] journaling

- [ ] baking a treat

- [ ] playing sports

- [ ] exercise

- [ ] taking a walk

- [ ] video games

☐ _____

☐ _____

☐ _____

☐ _____

☐ _____

Incorporating enjoyable activities into your life every day is a way to increase resilience against stress. Without fun activities, life can start to feel like it's an endless to-do list. Balancing out your life with things you enjoy helps increase your contentment with life. It is part building a life worth living.

It's important to allow yourself to fully enjoy the activities. If you are eating a snack but are worrying because it's not "healthy," or judge yourself for writing fan fiction, this adds to your stress rather than decreasing it.

You may feel you have to "earn" enjoyable activities, but not allowing yourself to do things you like can lead to burnout. You wouldn't keep driving a car with no gas and the check engine lights all on. Similarly, you can't run on stress and pressure alone.

Rosario is a senior and feeling stressed about the pressure to decide what she'll do after high school. She's also working a part-time job, and though it's fun, she feels pulled in a million different directions. Rosario is a big Taylor Swift fan, and she loves to look for Easter eggs in Taylor's music. While riding the bus to school and her job, she reads a Swiftie forum and posts her own theories. Rosario looks forward to reading these theories every day, and she's always in a good mood when she's spent time on the forum or journaling about clues in Taylor's lyrics.

FOR YOU TO DO

Reflect on the list of things that nourish you, and add any other activities you added at the bottom. Which are your favorites? Which are the most nourishing for you that usually put you in a good mood?

Are there any fun activities that you can add into your life? It can be from the previous list of fun activities or not—either is good. **Try adding one of these practices a day, and notice what happens.**

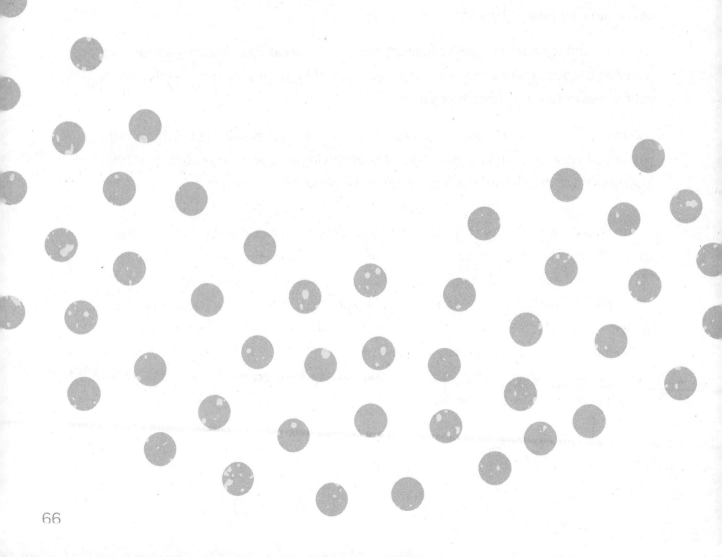

SECTION 14

SENSORY SYSTEMS AND REGULATION STRATEGIES

Most of us are familiar with the senses of sight, sound, hearing, touch, and taste, but there are three other senses it is useful to know about:

- *Proprioception* tells your body where it is in space. It helps with feeling grounded and moving smoothly.

- The *vestibular system* in your ears registers movement. It helps with balance and the stabilization of your posture and body.

- *Interoception* is the sense that lets you know when you are hungry, thirsty, in pain, need to use the bathroom, and other internal needs.

All humans have sensory needs. It is especially important for neurodivergent people to consider sensory needs, as they are more likely to have challenges with sensory input. This can be in the form of having greater sensitivity to sensory input (*hypersensitive*) or having less sensitivity (*hyposensitive*).

TOO MUCH OR TOO LITTLE INPUT?

It is common to have a mix of hypersensitivities and hyposensitivities. At times, having high sensitivity can be enjoyable! Some people love essential oils or trying different coffee varieties. They can sense the subtle differences that other people miss.

Other times, being sensitive to input can be painfully intense. We don't get to shut off our sensitivity and only notice pleasant things. You might get stressed in a grocery store with fluorescent lights and loud music. The smell of your lab partner's breakfast might make it difficult to concentrate on your assignment.

Hyposensitivity might sound nice compared to the overwhelm of noticing too much, but it has its own challenges. If you can't smell that food has gone bad, you can get sick. Tuning out dental pain can mean a small cavity becomes a much bigger problem. Sensory cues of pain or loud noise may not reach the level of conscious awareness but still impact your body and nervous system. Hunger causes physiological stress, even if you aren't aware of it until you're in tears because you need to eat *right now*.

MAKING SENSORY NEEDS WORK FOR YOU

Sensory experience can be a vulnerability factor. By taking your sensory needs seriously, you are reducing your vulnerabilities. Supporting sensory needs reduces stress and helps with emotional regulation. Adding in pleasant sensory experiences is a great way to create a life you enjoy.

Sensory needs can also fluctuate over time. Some people will report that certain things that bothered them when they were younger don't bother them now. This may be due to neurological development or simply being able to accommodate sensory needs better. For example, if acrylic fabrics bother you, when you get older, you can choose other clothes to wear.

Sensory needs can seem to increase at times of great stress. We are less able to tune out irritating things or tune into stimuli we tend to overlook. Hormonal changes—such as puberty, menstrual cycles, or hormone blockers or therapies—can also affect sensory experience.

Omar is an autistic sixteen-year-old. He likes his clothes to fit tight. Under his baggy hoodie, he likes to wear a snug thermal shirt. As a kid, Omar's grandmother noticed that bouncing calmed him down, so she got him a small trampoline. When Omar gets stressed by homework, he will use the trampoline to "help me think better." Engaging with a hyperfixation makes it harder for him to notice his weaker interoception cues, so his grandmother helped him make a plan to set an alarm when he is playing video games or doing homework to remind him to take a bathroom break and drink some water. The alarm has been helping a lot with Omar's sensory needs. Omar also loves heavy pressure, and laying under a weighted blanket while he watches true crime shows with his grandmother makes him happy and relaxed.

You may already be strongly aware of some preferences. It's important to attend to not just the sensory input you dislike but what you like as well. Knowing what feels good and making that a regular part of your life has a positive impact on your well-being. It can be a fun game to see how many sensory supports you can incorporate into your life!

Zora likes some weight on her head, so she tends to style her long hair in a bun on the crown of her head. Other times, she will wear her hair in a long braid because she likes the way it feels when she swings her head side to side. Zora incorporates each of the colors of the rainbow in her outfits, because "it's just so cheerful and loud!" She usually wears leggings, as she likes the pressure and the softness of the fabric.

FOR YOU TO DO

Fill out this sensory preferences self-assessment. Refer back to the beginning of this section if you need a reminder of what any of the senses involve.

SENSORY SYSTEM	WHAT I LIKE	WHAT I DON'T LIKE	WHAT I'M CURIOUS TO EXPLORE
TACTILE/TOUCH			
HEARING			
SIGHT			

TASTE			
SMELL			
PROPRIOCEPTION			
VESTIBULAR			
INTEROCEPTION			

What are some ways you already meet your sensory needs?

Are there ways you can increase pleasant sensory input? Are there ways you can eliminate or minimize bothersome sensory input?

WHEN TO GET SUPPORT

If hyposensitivities or hypersensitivities are causing significant challenges in your daily life, it might be helpful to speak to a professional. Your primary care provider can suggest referrals, such as an occupational therapist. Occupational therapists are trained to help people feel more comfortable with sensory input.

SECTION 15
SPECIAL INTERESTS

Special interests are subjects of intense interest and passion. They are often associated with autistic culture, but allistic (nonautistic) people can also have special interests as well. These interests can be lifelong, or they can be absorbing for just a few weeks. Anything can be the subject of a special interest: trains, TV shows, insects, historical costuming...you name it! People can have one special interest at a time, or they may have many.

At times, autistic people have been prevented from engaging in special interests, with the idea that special interests should be withheld as a reward for "good behavior." However, being prevented from engaging in a special interest can be very distressing. Other people have had their interests mocked and then feel embarrassed to engage in them. But many autistic people report that engaging in special interests is not only enjoyable, but important for emotional regulation and self-confidence. Research also backs up this lived experience. Special interests can also be a way to make social connections with others; many neurodivergent people find it easier to connect with people over a shared interest or activity, instead of talking with someone because you're the same age or in the same neighborhood.

Rowan has a special interest in makeup. When ze is feeling stressed, ze finds it helpful to take a break and play with eyeshadow. After engaging in zir special interest, ze feels refreshed and ready to reengage in the more challenging tasks ze needs to do. Ze says, "It helps me feel more 'me' when I do my makeup." Rowan even uses makeup as a mindfulness tool by focusing on the colors ze is using, noticing the feeling of the brushes and the scent of the makeup. Rowan has also made a few friends through chatting in the comments of makeup accounts online.

FOR YOU TO DO

Reflect on any special interests you have. What are they? If you don't currently have any, are there any special interests you have had in the past? Are there any subjects you want to explore?

What do you notice when you engage in your special interests? This could include thoughts, emotions, colors, words, and body sensations.

What are some ways you can engage in your special interest when feeling stressed?

Identify some ways you can regularly engage in your special interest.

SECTION 16
MASKING

Masking as a neurodivergent person means trying to hide your neurodivergence. This could look like:

- suppressing stimming—short for self-stimulation, which includes shaking your leg, using a fidget toy, or other behaviors that create sensory input for the brain—and body movements

- matching other people's facial expressions

- changing the way you speak, whether that is your tone, volume, or the words you use

- hiding your reactions to sensory input

- developing "scripts" to know what to say in different scenarios

- practicing facial expressions

- hiding your interests or how intense those interests are

You may think, "Everyone masks!" Of course, both neurotypical and neurodivergent people act differently in different situations. You might swear with your friends but not in class or in front of your grandmother. The difference with neurodivergent masking is that it goes beyond adjusting how you act based on the setting. It involves expectations that occur in almost all environments. If you have to smile and chat with customers at your job, you can probably get a break from that at home. But making eye contact is considered a norm in almost all Western contexts. You don't get a break from that just because you're off the clock.

When they have to mask, neurodivergent people are told that there is something wrong with who they are. It also tends to take a lot more effort for a neurodivergent person to mask their behavior. A neurotypical person doesn't have to think a lot about their facial expression, but a neurodivergent person may have to put a lot of effort into it. For some neurodivergent people, masking—such as by making eye contact or suppressing stimming—can feel physically painful or even impossible.

Sometimes masking is done consciously. You may have been told by adults or peers to stop acting a certain way, so you make sure to "act right." Other times, it's more subtle. You may have noticed that people aren't interested when you discuss your favorite show, so you stop bringing it up.

Gwen is a fourteen-year-old autistic teen. She's starting a new school and is hoping to make new friends. At Gwen's old school, her classmates would start side conversations and look at their phones when she would get focused on asking the teacher "too many" questions. She would sometimes rock in her seat when focusing hard but didn't realize it until her lab partner looked concerned and asked if Gwen was okay. Gwen watches a lot of British TV shows and used British slang until she realized it was confusing. Though no one told her she was being "weird" or "bad," she realized that she behaves very differently than her classmates. She wants to have close friends, so when her aunt said they were moving to a new town, she decided to try being "a normal teen." Gwen has figured out how to seem like she's making eye contact with someone without having to actually do it. She folds her arms tight across her chest. This helps her look bored and hides her urges to fidget. She has also figured out how to scrunch her toes inside her shoes when she needs to fidget secretly.

WHAT'S WRONG WITH MASKING, ANYWAY?

Sometimes masking is a matter of safety. Neurodivergent people have been punished for not meeting neurotypical standards. Fidgeting or not making eye contact can seem suspicious to others. Blending in with the group can be protective. (This strategy doesn't always work, however. Being bullied or abused happens because someone is choosing to bully, not because the victim is doing something wrong.)

People often engage in masking to meet their need for connection with others. Unfortunately, masking can make deeper connections difficult. It's hard to fully engage if you are focused on making sure your face looks "right" and that you're not talking about "weird stuff."

While masking might meet immediate needs, ongoing masking can lead to feeling like you don't know who you are. In the long term, it can contribute to depression. It's also exhausting! Sometimes people turn to risky coping mechanisms to handle the stresses of masking, such as substance use.

HOW TO UNMASK

Keep in mind that unmasking is an ongoing process. People often become more aware of masking behaviors over time. Try to have patience with yourself around unmasking.

Things to consider about unmasking:

- What are you like when you're alone? Do you dress differently? Do you move or speak differently?

- What were you like as a child or before you became more self-conscious? Family members may have stories if you can't remember.

- Connecting with other neurodivergent people, in person or online, can help give you examples of what unmasked people might look and act like.

- Experiment with new behaviors. For example, you might see what it's like to not make eye contact with people when speaking to them. Do you feel relieved? Is it easier to focus? Practice "infodumping" to a friend or even on a phone voice memo to see how it feels to talk for a long time about something you love. Let yourself express your excitement with your tone and body movements.

- Consider a safer place to unmask. You might consider family, a close friend, online spaces, or groups that work to be accepting. Neurodivergent people are everywhere, but some spaces seem to attract more neurodivergent folks. LGBTQ spaces, performing arts, and STEM activities are often neurodivergent friendly.

After a few months at her new school, **Gwen** is exhausted and miserable. Her aunt gives her a *Doctor Who* sticker and notices Gwen doesn't even put it on her water bottle. She speaks with Gwen about what is going on. Gwen shares her desire to "be normal," and her aunt expresses concerns about the toll this is taking. So, Gwen decides to post a notice in the school library for people who want to start a British TV fan club.

CONSCIOUSLY MASKING

At times, you may feel that you need or want to mask. If you're at a family event and your highly critical uncle is talking to you, it might be protective to mask your neurodivergence. Other times, you might decide that masking will help you meet your goals. Societal prejudices mean that people who appear more neurotypical are often seen as more credible. Imagine that your friend is making a sexual harassment claim against another student, and the school has asked to speak to you about an incident you witnessed. You might decide to engage in masking, in the hopes that will make you seem like a reliable witness. (You might also decide that you shouldn't have to hide being neurodivergent because of other people's prejudices and not mask.)

The important thing about these scenarios is that you are consciously choosing to mask. This does not take away all the negative impacts of masking, but being aware that you are masking gives you more agency.

How do you consciously mask?

- Use mindfulness skills to help you weigh pros and cons of masking.

- Remind yourself why you are engaging in masking. What goal or value does masking support?

- Remind yourself that masking is helpful or necessary because of society's prejudices. It is not because there is something wrong with the way you are.

- As much as possible, minimize the amount of time you spend masking.

- Have a plan for recovering afterward. Take a nap, engage with your special interests, journal—whatever will help you relieve stress.

FOR YOU TO DO

Do you engage in masking behaviors? What situations do you tend to mask in?

Are there places where you don't mask?

What are two masking behaviors that you could experiment with dropping? Consider the smallest step you could take. For example, you might not feel comfortable openly gushing about how amazing Afro Cuban jazz is, but you could stop pretending to be interested in pop music if you really hate it. Also, consider situations that are lower stakes for unmasking. It might be easier to practice not making eye contact when doing a small group project than it is when you're doing a presentation in front of the class. **Write out a plan for ways you can consciously unmask.**

PART 3

MINDFULNESS SKILLS

SECTION 17
STATES OF MIND

DBT often talks about states of mind. There are two basic ones we tend to operate in: *reason mind* and *emotion mind*. Both of these states have wisdom to share.

- **REASON, OR LOGIC MIND,** is "cool," focused on facts and tasks. This state is good for studying, planning, and analyzing.

- **EMOTION MIND** is "hot," ruled by urges and impulses. Your mood and emotional state dictate reality here. This state helps us act on our values even when they're not "practical."

You may usually be in one state more than another or move back and forth throughout the day. In chemistry class, you might be very focused on doing an experiment correctly. Later at lunch, you might sit with a friend and pass judgment on people based on their vibes.

However, each state in isolation has incomplete information. From a purely logical standpoint, no one should ever donate a kidney. It's a major surgical procedure. Donating a kidney does not directly benefit the donor. Thankfully, there are thousands of people each year who weigh the risks of donation and decide to do it anyway. They are moved to help someone they care about—or even a complete stranger. We all are faced with many more small-scale opportunities to do something kind or thoughtful for other people but that offers no direct benefit to us. Again, from a purely logical mind perspective, this could be foolish. But most of us enjoy being in a world where someone will hold open the door when we're carrying heavy boxes.

Being in purely emotion mind also has its downsides. If you break up with a friend and are feeling rejected and sad, it is not a good time to analyze what went wrong. You are probably not going to be able to calmly see a pattern of communication challenges you want to work on. It's much more likely that you will see everything through a lens of "I'm a terrible friend" and find evidence for why no one should ever or will ever be your friend again. Instead of solving the problem (if there is even a problem to solve!), you are left feeling more miserable.

Leticia is feeling intense fear around an upcoming school trip. It involves a long bus ride, and she keeps worrying about a car crash. Leticia is thinking of skipping school that day, even though her sister told her the field trip is really cool.

WISE MIND

A key goal in DBT is to bring the wisdom of both these states of mind together into the state of *wise mind*. Wise mind is not just about using our brain or our heart: it is connecting to the wisdom we all have inside of us. When we're in wise mind, we are not ignoring emotions or being ruled by them. We are considering facts but balancing them against other factors. Wise mind is personal. What one person's wise mind says may be very different from what yours tells you.

Being in wise mind:

- helps you have more control over your behavior

- gives you more choices about how to act

- reduces suffering

- helps you see multiple perspectives

- increases your self-trust

- reconnects you to your core self after invalidation around neurodivergence

When you're in wise mind, you might recognize that you're angry at your teacher about your grade but that yelling isn't going to help the situation. Instead, you might vent to your mom after school, and wise mind might help you see that it would be better to talk to your teacher when you're less angry. Or perhaps wise mind would help you recognize that while you're angry about your grade, you also consistently turned in assignments late. In this case, wise mind might lead you to problem solve about how to meet deadlines.

The rest of part 3 focuses on mindfulness practices, which show you how to build a relationship with your own wise mind. It can be easy to think we're in wise mind, especially when we are actually still in emotion mind. For example, you might have a "gut feeling" that sounds like wise mind. Upon later reflection, you might realize it was your anxiety falsely telling you that a situation was unsafe. Accessing wise mind can be even more challenging for neurodivergent people, who have been told for many years that they are wrong. Over time, this erodes self-trust. Learning to find wise mind helps you reconnect with your inner knowing.

After a good night's sleep, **Leticia** tries to look at the field trip from a purely logical perspective. She thinks that if the trip was truly life threatening, the school wouldn't allow it. They wouldn't want to risk a lawsuit. She does some research and finds out that fatalities from school bus accidents are very rare and that in fact school buses are much safer than cars. While Leticia is still worried, she has some facts to counterbalance what her emotion mind is telling her.

FOR YOU TO DO

What are signs you're in emotion mind? What about logic mind?

Think of a recent situation that felt somewhat intense or confusing. When trying new skills, it's easier to work with a situation that is not the most intense you have ever felt. For example, it could be easier to reflect on someone flirting with you and you not being sure how to handle it rather than finding out you failed three classes. Consider this situation through an emotion mind perspective.

Write or draw what emotion mind tells you about this perspective.

Now consider it from logic mind. Write or draw what you see from a logic mind stance.

Bring the two together. What does each perspective add?

SECTION 18

MINDFULNESS AS A NEURODIVERGENT PERSON

Mindfulness has become a big buzzword in recent years. You may have encountered mindfulness exercises in school or even explored the practice on your own. For many neurodivergent people, the idea of mindfulness is off-putting. You might think you have to sit quietly on a cushion with no thoughts in your head. That can seem impossible for many neurodivergent teens, whose brains and bodies are constantly in motion. Fortunately, there are many ways to be mindful.

What exactly is mindfulness, anyway? The idea of sitting on a cushion and calmly focusing on your breath is one form of mindfulness—one that falls under the umbrella of meditation. But mindfulness is bigger than just mediation. Mindfulness simply means the practice of being aware of what is happening in the present moment: what is happening around us, as well as our internal sensations and thoughts.

While it is helpful at times to reflect on the past and to plan for the future, being too caught up in the past or present takes away from our current experience. Most of us have had the experience of worrying about something coming up—a driver's license exam or a hard conversation with a friend—and not being able to enjoy anything before the dreaded event. We miss out on enjoying life as it is happening right now. Of course, life is not always enjoyable! But mindfulness can help with that as well.

BENEFITS OF MINDFULNESS

- **Increased awareness of thoughts and judgments that are below the level of conscious awareness.** Many people have a mean and judgmental commentary about themselves running in their heads. If you are not fully aware of these thoughts, a repeated script of "there you go again, being stupid" running in your head affects your mental and emotional well-being.

- **Increased awareness of subtle physical or emotional cues.** These make it easier to address things like early signs of hunger—*before* you are in tears from not eating for most of the day. These benefits are especially important for people who have challenges with interoception and alexithymia (see sections 14 and 22 for more information).

- **Pausing before reacting.** You can respond intentionally instead of reacting based on assumptions or intense emotions.

- **Staying focused on the present instead of running off with worry.** Just having a fight with a good friend is hard enough without spiraling into worries that you will never have friends again or that everyone secretly hates you.

- **Getting more out of pleasant experiences in life.** Whether it's a tasty chocolate bar, a favorite book, or a fun outing with your family, it can feel like good things go by too quickly. While we can't actually create more time, we can get more *out* of our time by being present to enjoy it as it is happening.

Sometimes people are wary of mindfulness because they think the aim is to take away your emotions or personality. Mindfulness is not meant to take away your emotions. Instead, it gives you more choices about how you respond to challenging situations—whether they come from outside of yourself or from your own thoughts and emotions. Mindfulness can help increase your effectiveness.

Parneet has an accommodation that allows her to leave class a few minutes before the end of the period. This allows her to get to her next class before the hallways become crowded and overwhelming. Her second period teacher often has her stay until the end of the class, even when Parneet wants to leave early. Parneet gets angry when her teacher has these responses, and there have been several times when she has yelled at the teacher. Parneet has gotten two referrals because of this. After regular mindfulness practice, Parneet has been able to hold back on yelling at her teacher. Instead, she's been keeping track of these incidents to have a record. When her teacher tries to prevent her from leaving class early, Parneet takes a moment and calmly states, "My 504 says I can go early," and she quietly leaves the classroom.

Parneet's anger at being denied her accommodations is justified, but her explosive reactions are not effective. Her behavior may undermine her valid complaint. Through mindfulness practice, Parneet was able to make more effective choices about how to use her anger to get her needs met.

PRACTICING MINDFULNESS

Try a number of different practices to see what you actually like. Don't dismiss mindfulness out of hand, saying things like, "Meditation just doesn't work for a busy ADHD brain." The truth is that while mediation may be harder for some brains than others, it is generally difficult for all people. And you can practice mindfulness without ever meditating! The more active your brain is, the more you may actually benefit from a mindfulness practice. Something may be difficult *and* also worth trying (there's that dialectical thinking again!).

When you are experimenting with mindfulness, it is worth trying a method several times before you decide it does not work for you. You may need to try it a different time of day, in a different location, or with a different focus. For example, if you are practicing mindfully listening to music, you might try it with music you are familiar with versus music that is new to you. The rest of part 3 will give further information on how to practice mindfulness.

FOR YOU TO DO

What are your thoughts and assumptions about mindfulness?

Do you have any experience with practicing mindfulness? Thinking about mindfulness as simply the practice of being present, are there any things you already do that you can recognize as a mindfulness practice (e.g. drawing, stretching, or playing with a fidget toy)?

SECTION 19
OBSERVE AND DESCRIBE

"Observe" and "describe" are two fundamental DBT skills. They're useful for gaining clarity and not running away with assumptions.

J wants to try a new trick at the skate park. They've watched a lot of YouTube videos and feel ready to give it a try. When they go to the park on Saturday, they are excited but nervous. However, the trick turns out to be much harder than they expected, and they're feeling frustrated because they just can't get it. J notices some kids at the skate park laughing and thinks they might be laughing at them. J feels angry and embarrassed. A girl from school says hi in a friendly way, and J thinks she's taking pity on them for being such a loser who can't get a trick right.

"Observing" simply means noticing without judgment or taking action. We observe what is in the present without making predictions about the future or ruminating on the past. Many mindfulness exercises are focused on observing.

What can we actually observe?

- our thoughts

- our feelings

- things other people say

- sensory details

- anything that could be recorded by a camera

Note that we can't observe other people's thoughts and feelings, except for what they share with us. J's assumption that their classmate is being nice because she pities them is an assumption, not an actual observation.

"Describing" involves putting words to what we observe. It is important to use language that is as specific as possible. For example, if you say, "My mom is so ridiculous about cleaning," that does not actually convey much information about your mom. The word "ridiculous" is a judgment that captures your thoughts about the subject. A more descriptive statement will paint a picture. It might look like this:

"My mom has an 80s playlist she puts on Saturday mornings when we clean the house. She wears this retro tracksuit and tells us what a 'rad' job we're doing. I think it's ridiculous."

WHY USE THESE SKILLS

- They help us see what's happening more clearly.

- They help us not run away with painful assumptions.

Returning to J, they could use these observe and describe skills to say, "I am having the thought that my classmate is being nice because she feels sorry for me." They could notice that their classmate came across the skate park to say something to J and that she smiled at them. J could be right that she pities them, but they don't know that for sure. Noticing this can help stop J from adding to their story about how they are a loser and everyone else thinks so. This alone can prevent a lot of emotional pain.

Recognizing your thoughts and emotions as simply thoughts and emotions rather than "the truth" also allows a little distance from them. Consider the following statements:

- I'm going to fail this test.

- I'm having the thought that I'm going to fail this test.

The first one is stated more as a matter of truth. Failing the test is a determined outcome. In the second statement, the phrase "I'm having the thought" creates a gap to recognize that this is not necessarily the truth. It is just a thought. This can prevent you from snowballing into a story about failing the test that leads to increased stress and anxiety. (And of course, being stressed and anxious is not likely to help you on the test!)

Our thoughts and feelings are real and important to acknowledge. And they are not the complete truth. Remembering this can help us be less reactive. Imagine that J believes their classmate is pitying them or even mocking them. J might yell at their classmate. They might also avoid the class they share, thinking, "I can't be in the same room with someone who knows what a loser I am." Both of these are strong reactions to something that may not even be true.

FOR YOU TO DO

EXERCISE OBSERVING AND DESCRIBING

Practice observing and describing something you feel neutral or positive about. Things you feel neutral or positive about are often easier to begin practicing with because there is less emotional charge. You could try using these skills to describe an animal, a song you like, or your favorite outfit. Focus on identifying your thoughts and emotions, as well as the sensory details of what you are observing.

Lourdes is petting her pet cat, Barney. She notices her cat is warm from sleeping in the sun. Lourdes observes the way the stripes on his back break up into spots on his belly. She has the thought that Barney is her favorite cat and notices how calm her body feels when she pets him.

SECTION 20

SENSORY-FOCUSED MINDFULNESS PRACTICES

Using sensory experiences as a focus for meditation can be helpful for times when internal focus feels too difficult or even emotionally painful. Focusing on input from our physical environment can help orient and ground us to the here and now.

Sensory-focused mindfulness can be especially enjoyable for neurodivergent people. If you are hypersensitive to sensory input, these exercises can increase enjoyment in your daily life. Listening to a piece of music you love and feeling like you are becoming one with the instruments can be a source of great joy. This is also helpful for people trying to develop more of a sense of their inner experiences. These exercises can be brief, but their impact adds up over time.

FOR YOU TO DO

Practice using your senses to engage in mindfulness. Here are two example practices to get you started:

EXERCISE MINDFUL HANDWASHING

Washing your hands is something you do multiple times a day. When you wash your hands, practice observing and describing that experience.

You might note the temperature of the water and how strong or weak the water pressure is. Take a moment to be aware of the scent of the soap and the feel of it on your hands. Notice the sound of the water flowing and the silence after the water is turned off.

EXERCISE SENSE-BASED GROUNDING

Ground yourself in your environment using your five senses.

1. Notice five things you can see around you.

2. Next, identify four things you can touch, and imagine the texture of those objects.

3. Listen for three noises you can hear.

4. Try to identify two different scents in your environment.

5. Finally, notice one thing you can taste.

Now, identify one thing that could work as a focus for mindfulness for each sense. **What's one thing you observed that you could focus in on, observing and describing it the way you did in the handwashing exercise?**

Sight: _____

Touch: _____

Hearing: _____

Scent: _____

Taste: _____

SECTION 21
RADICAL ACCEPTANCE

Radical acceptance means acknowledging what is happening in the current moment without judging or fighting it. It is a mindfulness skill that can be hard to put into practice.

Radical acceptance does not mean:

- you like what is happening

- you have to be okay with how things are

- what is happening is good and optimal

- you are minimizing what is going on

- nothing will ever change

- you should give up

It just means acknowledging things as they currently are.

WHY RADICALLY ACCEPT?

First, we need to clearly see what is going on. Avoiding reality or saying things should be different won't change what is happening.

Carolyn's school requires passing two PE classes to graduate. Carolyn hates PE and "anything exercise related." She failed PE freshman year and did not sign up for a PE class the next year. Carolyn is avoiding meeting with her counselor to register for junior year classes because she knows her counselor will say she needs to take PE.

Carolyn is avoiding the reality of her graduation requirements. As a result of not accepting that she needs to take PE classes, she is stressed about class registration. She may also not graduate from high school. Eventually, Carolyn will be forced to deal with the PE requirement. The longer she delays, the more likely it is to become a crisis.

Accepting the PE requirement does not mean that Carolyn has to suddenly love exercise! It just means she has to acknowledge that the requirement exists.

Sometimes, accepting what is happening allows us to ultimately make change that is more effective. Carolyn can try to make alternate arrangements, get her GED, or accept that if she wants to graduate, she needs to pass PE classes.

Often, the lack of acceptance increases suffering. We get caught up in what "should be" and feel anger, fear, sadness, or avoidance. Meanwhile, the situation that is upsetting us continues. We are not able to move on if we are stuck on what we think should be happening.

HOW TO PRACTICE RADICAL ACCEPTANCE

First, radical acceptance is very difficult to do for all people! And it can be especially difficult for neurodivergent people, whose identities are often centered on strong values or a strong drive for justice. It can feel like accepting what is happening is just giving in and saying things are fine as they are. Radical acceptance can also be hard if you are a perfectionist. Often, there is no perfect answer to life's problems.

> Carolyn's school counselor pulls her from class to register for next year. When he reminds her of the PE requirement, she starts ranting about it. Her counselor acknowledges she does not want to take PE but that it is required. He tells Carolyn, "You're fighting reality."

Sometimes radical acceptance is a temporary step toward change, sometimes it's something we cannot change—and sometimes it's both.

The first step to radical acceptance is to notice that you are fighting reality. Try accepting the situation with your mind by saying, "This is what is happening." Accept with your body as well. If you are saying, "Yes, this is true," but crossing your arms and scowling, you are not radically accepting. Practice mindfulness of your thoughts and emotions, as well as your physical sensation. You could repeat a phrase to yourself to help accept reality. It is likely that you will have to do this over and over.

> Carolyn reluctantly agrees that she wants to graduate from high school. She discusses different options with her counselor, and he places her in a first period PE class. This way she will get the class over with and not have to dread it for the whole day. In the fall, when Carolyn heads into her PE class, she pauses and reminds herself, "This is what is gonna get me on that stage." She imagines herself accepting her diploma. She still doesn't like PE, but she participates enough to pass the class.

RADICAL ACCEPTANCE AND JUSTICE SENSITIVITY

Many neurodivergent people are especially sensitive to issues of justice, fairness, and equity. These are wonderful qualities that make our world a better place! But they can also be places where we get bogged down. In addition, many neurodivergent people tend toward perfectionism. Being able to have a large-scale vision is wonderful; beating yourself up because you can't fully achieve that vision by yourself is not. Doing what you can may not be enough to solve a problem, but it's still worth doing. After all, larger problems can only be solved by many people engaging in a variety of actions.

Yaw is a sixteen-year-old autistic teen who has been struggling with depression. He feels despair over the state of the world and is especially worried about the environment. He wishes that world leaders would take the problem seriously. He talks to his therapist, who encourages him to identify what he can do. Yaw decides to advocate for reducing food waste at school and starting a composting system. He begins researching programs at other schools and collecting statistics from the cafeteria staff about food waste from his school. He is working on a presentation to make to the school board about composting. His biology teacher even offered extra credit for this project. Yaw still worries about climate change and still wishes more people would take action. He continues to practice accepting that he is doing what he can.

Much about our lives is out of our control. As a teen, you are legally dependent on your caregivers. You likely have little choice over where you live or go to school. Your family may require you to do certain things, such as participate in family dinners. Or they may prevent you from doing things you would like to, such as dating. We are all subject to laws and forces that are outside of our control.

Sometimes all that is within our control is how we think and respond to what is happening. For example, you have no control over your parents' choice to divorce. But you can open up to your youth group leader instead of burying your feelings about it. Fighting against the reality of the divorce will get you nowhere. The first step is to accept that it is happening. From there, you can take action, such as getting support, and work to continue accepting the new reality as it unfolds.

FOR YOU TO DO

Does the idea of radical acceptance bring up strong feelings for you? What do you think about this idea?

Is there an area where radical acceptance would be helpful for you? What is the first step you can take to radically accept?

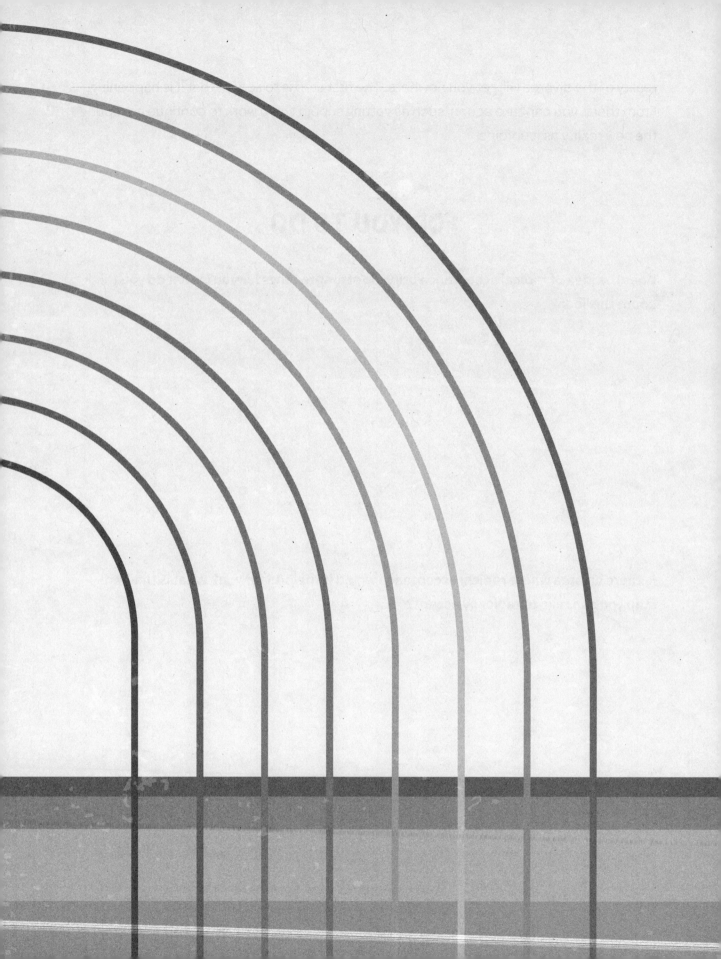

PART 4

RIDING THE WAVES OF EMOTION

SECTION 22
APPRECIATING EMOTIONS

Emotions give color to life. Imagine reading a sweeping epic like *The Lord of the Rings* and being completely unmoved by Frodo's journey. Or imagine listening to a technical genius play the guitar but with no emotional tone. Something would be lacking from the experience. Even an emotion we usually find unpleasant, like grief, is a sign of how much we cared about what is now lost.

In a DBT framework, emotions serve several important purposes:

- **THEY COMMUNICATE THINGS TO US.** Guilt lets us know we've done something that goes against our values. Happiness helps us recognize what we enjoy.

- **THEY GET US READY TO ACT.** Fear alerts us to danger. Anger gives us motivation to advocate for our rights.

- **THEY COMMUNICATE TO OTHERS AND INFLUENCE THEM.** When others can tell we are happy, they know we liked the movie they chose. If people react with disgust when you pick your nose in public, it lets you know that is outside social norms.

Emotional experiences are not just about *what* emotion we're feeling but how intense that feeling is. Happiness can range from a brief moment of enjoyment at seeing a cute dog to feeling like your heart is going to explode with joy when you find out your family will be adopting that cute dog.

Sometimes we have been told our emotions are "too much," and we tune them down. You might tell yourself to not get so excited about something. Or sometimes, they are too painful for us, so we cut them off entirely. There are some families and communities where only certain emotions are acceptable. Gratitude might be the only thing you are allowed to express. Anger is considered unacceptable from many people in our society, but for others, such as men, it's often the only emotion that's "okay" to express. The problem is that when you avoid one type of emotion, or suppress the intensity of that emotion, it tends to have a deadening effect. Doing so can lead to numbness. Feeling too little is as much of a problem as feeling too much.

EMOTIONAL REGULATION

Emotional regulation is the ability to have control over your emotional state. We'll explore how to do this in the rest of part 4. It's important to know that the point of these skills is not to turn you into a robot who is always happy, nor to get rid of emotions. *All* emotions are important. Rather, emotional regulation skills are meant to give you more options for responding. They also help increase your effectiveness. Imagine buying something at a store and later realizing the clerk accidentally rang up an item twice. What will be more effective at getting you a refund? Storming into the store, swearing and threatening to fight the clerk for cheating you? Or going into the store and saying, "I was overcharged here. I need a refund."

The goal is not to always have your emotions set on a medium setting! Sometimes, expressing intensity is useful. If a doctor is not taking your symptoms seriously, pressing them with some urgency can help you get the medical care you need. Calmly saying, "My side kinda hurts," may not convey the seriousness of your symptoms. You may have to amplify your expression of distress. (On the other hand, screaming and hitting the doctor when they are trying to examine you may get in the way of getting care! The trick is to have the right amount of intensity.)

It's important to understand that while our emotions are genuine and should be taken seriously, emotions aren't the sole judge of truth. (There's that dialectical thinking again!) That's why wise mind combines both emotions and logic. If you feel angry when someone bumps into you in the hallway, that doesn't mean the person is trying to hurt you. You may feel guilty about not calling your grandmother more often, but that doesn't mean she is trying to make you feel guilty. Your feelings are valid, but the conclusions you draw from them may not be accurate. This is a good time to practice mindfulness of thoughts: "My brain is telling me I'm unlovable. It's just a thought."

Emotions can also be confusing because we often react to the past rather than what is right in front of us—that's why it's useful to engage wise mind and check the facts. We'll explore evaluating the facts along with emotions in section 24.

WHAT MAKES IT HARD TO REGULATE EMOTIONS?

- **BIOLOGY.** Some people have innately higher highs and lower lows or are more easily activated into more intense emotions. Mood disorders can make emotions more intense as well.

- **VULNERABILITY FACTORS.** Being hungry, tired, sick, or under a lot of stress makes everything more difficult!

- **TRAUMA.** Responding to the past as if it's happening now makes emotions stronger than they normally would be. A sudden loud noise might be startling, but if you had previously witnessed a shooting, it might send you into a panic.

- **ALEXITHYMIA.** Not being able to recognize emotions makes it difficult to regulate them! We'll discuss alexithymia more later.

- **REJECTION SENSITIVITY.** This can cause emotions to come on quick and strong. We'll discuss rejection sensitivity more in a later section.

- **LACK OF SKILL.** Simply not having the tools needed to regulate emotions.

- **EXTREME EMOTIONS.** These can keep going on and on. Have you ever gotten into a crying jag where you just keep crying more and more? Or been so angry that everything makes you angrier, even things that would normally not bother you?

- **SENSITIVITY TO OTHERS' EMOTIONS.** If you're picking up a lot from the environment, it can be harder to regulate emotions—after all, you are feeling bombarded by the emotions of other people too.

- **REINFORCEMENT.** Intense emotions can be accidentally reinforced by the people around us. Babies tend to give a small cry when they are hungry. If these small cries go unheard, the baby will escalate until they're screaming, which usually brings caregivers running. If this pattern happens repeatedly, the baby might learn that screaming is the only effective way to get food, so they'll start with screaming right off the bat. In similar ways, we can get reinforced to express intense emotions to get the attention and support that we need. It's important to recognize that this behavior is created by the interaction between the environment and the person. Often, this pattern is blamed solely on the baby who learns to scream right away. The baby or person who learned such a pattern is often labeled "manipulative" or "dramatic," which is unfair.

- **FAULTY BELIEFS.** People might think that intense emotions are the most "real" or have other beliefs, such as, "If I don't feel guilty all the time, I will turn into a selfish monster."

FOR YOU TO DO

Do you like having emotions or would you turn them off if you could?

Which emotions are you more comfortable with? What emotions are hard for you?

Identify three things you would like to be different about your relationship to emotions.

SECTION 23

WHAT EMOTION AM I FEELING?

The first step in emotion regulation is knowing what emotion you are feeling, which is often easier said than done—knowing your emotions can actually be very tricky, especially for neurodivergent people.

Alexithymia is a personality trait that makes it difficult for people to identify their emotions. People of all neurotypes can have alexithymia, but it's more common for autistic people and ADHDers. An estimated 50 percent of autistic people are alexithymic.

Alexithymia can also develop with other types of neurodivergence. For example, people with depression or PTSD can become numb to their emotions. When the depression or trauma is treated, the alexithymia tends to go away.

Whether you're born with alexithymia or it develops later, you can become better at identifying emotions. It's worth developing these skills, as alexithymia can cause significant challenges. These may include:

- **CHALLENGES IN RELATIONSHIPS.** If you struggle to identify your own emotions, it is often hard to identify others' emotions as well. This can be misinterpreted as not caring about the other person. It can lead to conflict or even relationships ending.

- **CONSEQUENCES OF SLOWER PROCESSING.** People with alexithymia typically require a lot of mental processing to identify emotions. This takes time! You may realize later that your initial reaction to something was not your real reaction. You might find yourself saying, "I laughed, but it really hurt my feelings." Sometimes people feel they are not allowed to "change their feelings" like this. Other people may judge you as flaky.

- **NOT HAVING IMPORTANT INFORMATION.** Emotions can be cues to act. For example, fear lets us know when there is a potential threat. Anger can let us know when our rights are being violated. If we cannot identify our emotions, we are missing valuable information.

- **BIG REACTIONS "OUT OF NOWHERE."** Stressors can pile up on an alexithymic person without them realizing. Then, when something exceeds their stress threshold, they suddenly respond to *everything* that has been happening. Imagine a day where you are late to school, you have a surprise quiz, and the cafeteria is out of your favorite food. Without being aware of these stressors, you cannot take steps to let the stress go or soothe yourself. Then your sibling eats the snack you were looking forward to. All the pent-up stress of the day hits, and you end up screaming at your sibling.

- **IMPACTS ON SELF-IMAGE.** Having emotions that seem changeable or intense reactions can take a toll on your self-esteem. People with alexithymia often judge themselves harshly: "Why am I so out of control?"

- **EMOTIONAL ROLLERCOASTER.** Often alexithymic people do not recognize their emotions until they become very intense. This can be exhausting! It also makes using emotional regulation skills challenging. It is harder to deal with feelings when they are at a 10/10 in intensity, versus a 4/10 or even a 7/10.

- **RISKY BEHAVIORS.** Alexithymia is associated with higher rates of harmful coping behaviors such as self-harm, substance abuse, and eating disorders. These risky behaviors change emotional states quickly. When your emotions are at 10/10 intensity, it can feel relieving to drop that intensity in a matter of minutes. Unfortunately, these coping behaviors are dangerous and even life threatening.

Yumi is a seventeen-year-old autistic teen with alexithymia. She and her boyfriend Peter often fight because Yumi is frequently unsure about her feelings. Peter wonders if she is actually in love with him. Yumi's friends get frustrated with her because sometimes she will laugh at their jokes and later come back and express hurt at some of those jokes. Yumi acknowledges that it's hard when she does not know her feelings.

There are many tools to help with alexithymia:

- Simply being aware of it can be helpful! Remind yourself that challenges with emotional identification are not a moral failure but a personality trait. If you know it takes a while to access emotions, you can plan to take a pause before reacting.

- If it feels safe to do so, you may disclose to others that you are alexithymic. You can share a lot: "I'm an ADHDer with alexithymia, and this is what it looks like for me..." or a little: "I'm not sure how I feel about that, I'll have to think about it."

- Mindfulness helps you build a map of your internal world. Many people find practices such as yoga useful for increasing awareness of their emotions.

- Reflecting on your past experiences can be helpful—if something similar happened to you before, how did you feel about it later? Sometimes, taking the question outside of yourself can make things clearer. Ask yourself, "What is someone likely to feel in this situation?" You could also reflect on how friends, family, or characters in a TV show would respond.

- You can also work on mapping your emotional landscape by using your observe and describe skills to notice what the prompting event was and what thoughts, feelings, and body sensations you are having. What emotions do you think you might be having? Are there clues in the thoughts you are having? Keeping a journal of these responses can help you learn the ways that your emotions show up. The following chart has some common experiences associated with emotions to help you get started.

EMOTION	WHAT MIGHT LEAD TO THE EMOTION	BODY CHANGES THAT MAY OCCUR	WAYS YOU MIGHT EXPRESS THE EMOTION
ANGER	Physical or emotional pain; being attacked; things not turning out as you hoped; believing you are completely right and others are wrong; thinking about people that have wronged you	Feeling hot; clenching or gritting your teeth; wanting to hit, shove, or punch; tears	Yelling; hitting; "huffing" your breath; stomping; frowning; crying; criticizing; blaming
FEAR	Being in a new situation; trauma flashbacks; sensing a threat; thoughts of being hurt or rejected	Physically "freezing"; racing heart; nausea; wanting to run; shaking	Crying; running away; shaking; diarrhea or vomiting; feeling stuck in place
HAPPINESS	Meeting a goal; being with people who truly like you; enjoyable sensory input	Feeling calm; having a lot of energy; laughing	Jumping up and down; smiling; enjoying stimming; laughing
SADNESS	A loss; feeling isolated; thinking about problems in the world; worst case scenarios happening; thoughts of hopelessness or worthlessness	Tiredness; crying; frowning; feelings of emptiness	Crying; sobbing; avoiding people or things you normally enjoy; withdrawing; staying silent

SHAME	Rejection, invalidation, or criticism—or the threat of these events; "messing up"	Hiding; slumping; avoiding others; stomachache	Hiding; overapologizing; avoiding the people or places that trigger shame
GUILT	Violating your values; not keeping promises; hurting yourself or another; blaming yourself	Feeling hot; having a hard time breathing	Apologizing; trying to fix the problem; avoidance

FOR YOU TO DO

Do your emotions show up in these ways? Are there ways your feelings present differently?

Are there emotions that are easier for you to identify? Which emotions are harder to detect?

SECTION 24
WORKING WITH EMOTIONS

Knowing when and how to act on emotions can be hard, especially for neurodivergent people, who have long been told their reactions are wrong. It can be difficult to know when it's "okay" to feel sad, angry, or even happy, much less what to do about it. The DBT skills in this section can help you evaluate your feelings and make the best decisions you can.

First, when you notice an emotion, you can simply let the emotion be. Not every feeling needs deep analysis. You can also use your emotion as a focus for mindfulness, identifying what it feels like in your body and noticing how it shifts over time. (This can be especially helpful if you're working with alexithymia.)

However, if the emotion is

- persistent,

- very strong,

- distressing, or

- urging you to take action,

then it's worth engaging wise mind to assess what you want to do.

If your emotions are running very high and causing you to feel panicky or totally overwhelmed, skip ahead to section 26, "Coping Through Strong Emotions." The skills in this current section are best used when you are not in the highest levels of distress. On a scale where 0 is "totally calm" and 10 is "totally freaked out," use the skills in this section when you're at a 7 or below.

CHECKING THE FACTS

Once your emotional intensity has been determined or even decreased, you can start checking the facts to get more information about your emotions and if you want to take action on them.

Life can be very painful. If your cat is your best friend, losing her will be sad no matter what. But often, our suffering is increased by our thoughts. If your cat dies and you think, "I will never have a friend again, I will be lonely forever," you will probably feel more miserable than if you just sat with your sadness about her death. Sometimes, suffering is entirely caused by thoughts and interpretations. If you think everyone at the grocery store is focusing on you and thinking how disgusting you are, you're likely to feel pretty horrible—entirely based on your assumptions about other people's thoughts.

It's also worth checking the facts because we only have our own perspectives on things. Thinking we have the absolute truth can lead to suffering. Remember dialectics: two seemingly opposite things can be true at the same time. Your friend could hurt your feelings by canceling plans, *and* she may be burned out and in need of rest. Feeling sad or disappointed by this makes sense, *and* verbally attacking your friend for being a selfish jerk will probably not make her want to reschedule with you.

To begin with checking the facts, first you need to know what it is you are feeling. Once you have identified that, or at least have a good guess, then try to identify what happened to start the emotion. It could be something that happened outside of you—your friend canceling plans—or inside of you. For example, maybe your friend mentioned that she's really burned out, but she didn't cancel plans with you. If you think she's hinting she wants to cancel and you start feeling angry and sad about it, the precipitating event would be "my friend said she was tired, and I started thinking she is going to cancel and that it's a personal rejection."

Use observe and describe skills to name the facts of the situation. In the situation of a friend who canceled on you, look for the facts. Remember, facts are:

- what you observe through your senses

- based in observation and description

Some facts about the situation might include: "She was looking at her phone when she canceled our plans," "She texted me ten minutes before we were supposed to meet," and "She mentioned in algebra she could sleep for the whole weekend." The following statements, however, are *not* facts: "She canceled and didn't even care," "She's a flake," and "No one wants to be my friend." They are interpretations and assumptions.

Once you've determined the facts, look now at the interpretations you are making. Mindfully using phrases like "I had the thought that" can help you recognize your statements as your thoughts (not necessarily the truth). "She texted me ten minutes before we were supposed to meet, so I thought she just didn't care about my feelings" is more mindful and regulating than running away with the story: "She texted me ten minutes before we were supposed to meet because she doesn't care about my feelings. She's so selfish, and I'm dumb for being friends with her."

Consider other interpretations of the facts. It's possible that, if your friend repeatedly cancels on you, she might not be invested in your relationship. However, it could also be that your friend is struggling and doing the best she can. Maybe your friend feels secure enough in your relationship that she can be honest with you and rest when she needs to. Which interpretations fit the facts better?

It's worth noting that your initial interpretations may be correct! Your friend may indeed be trying to gently ghost you. But it's better to come at that understanding from considering both the facts and your feelings rather than feelings alone.

If you do come up with an interpretation that better fits the facts than your first take, it doesn't invalidate your feelings. There still may be something you want to address in the situation. If your friend cancels plans at the last minute and you feel rejected, but later realize that your friend is struggling with autistic burnout, you're not "bad" for feeling sad about the canceled plans. The shift in interpretation can help guide how intense your response is. If you think your friend is trying her best to manage a hard situation, you'll likely be gentler with her than if you believe she doesn't care about your feelings at all.

HOW INTENSE SHOULD YOUR FEELINGS BE?

Once you've determined that your emotion fits the facts, you need to next consider whether the intensity of your emotion fits the facts as well. Sometimes our emotions are too intense for what has happened. If your friend cancels on you and you're sad or angry, that makes sense. If you were looking forward to spending time with your friend, it is probably disappointing or frustrating that she canceled. If you have a hard time adapting to change, the last-minute change itself might be irritating. If you're so angry that you want to punch your friend in the face, however, that's too strong of a response. (Punching your friend is also likely to lead to more problems.)

On the other hand, our emotions can also be too understated. Imagine your friend is constantly canceling on you, only reaching out when she needs to borrow money she never pays back. In that case, feeling mild annoyance toward your friend might not be a strong enough emotion to motivate you to address it or even end a relationship that feels too transactional.

Is There a Threat?

If you have checked the facts and emotions are still really high, it's worth considering if you are assuming a threat. Naming it can help—maybe you're afraid that you will *never* have a friend again. Reflect on how likely that is. While friends aren't truly replaceable or interchangeable, it's hard to imagine that you will never find another friend as long as you live. You may also discover that the threat, whatever it may be, is real. In that case, you are clearer about the situation and can take more effective action.

FOR YOU TO DO

Practice checking the facts. It might be easier to start with a situation that evokes a moderate emotional response. If your family pet recently died, it might be too intense of a situation to practice with. If you are sad but find it manageable—maybe your pet died a while ago—it might be a good example for skills practice. You could even practice by using a situation from a work of fiction.

WHAT EMOTION ARE YOU FEELING? (If answering this is challenging, use the emotion chart in section 23.)	
HOW INTENSE ARE YOUR EMOTIONS? (If they are at a 7/10 or above, or if they feel overwhelming, use the tools in section 26.)	
WHEN YOUR EMOTIONS ARE LESS INTENSE, CONSIDER THE FACTS. WHAT CAN YOU OBSERVE THROUGH YOUR SENSES?	

WHAT ASSUMPTIONS, INTERPRETATIONS, AND JUDGMENTS ARE YOU MAKING?	
WHAT ARE SOME OTHER INTERPRETATIONS MIGHT FIT THE FACTS?	
ARE YOUR EMOTIONS STILL HIGH? (If so, what is the threat you are perceiving? How likely is the threat to happen? How could you cope if it did happen?)	

SECTION 25

PROBLEM SOLVE OR ACT OPPOSITE

Sometimes just the act of checking the facts helps with our emotions. We might recognize we've gotten off track with assumptions or interpretations. We may have identified a perceived threat that is making our emotional response more intense and evaluated that threat.

However, sometimes we realize after checking the facts that emotions are prompting us to take action. Or the feelings might continue to cause us pain, whether or not they fit the facts. What to do with these feelings?

DBT offers two pathways:

- **PROBLEM SOLVING** is taking steps to change the situation. It is used when your emotion fits the facts and taking action is effective. If you feel guilty because you ate the candy you knew your brother was saving, you might problem solve by apologizing and replacing the candy.

- **OPPOSITE ACTION** means going against what your emotions are telling you to do. It is used when the emotion fits the facts but acting on it isn't effective. If you hurt your friend, feeling some guilt might make sense. However, if your friend has said "never speak to me again," calling to apologize will not help the situation. Sometimes, acting on emotions can make a situation worse. Opposite action is also useful for when your emotions do *not* fit the facts. You might feel guilty if you get the starting pitcher position and your friend was cut from the team. You might think you should quit the team to not hurt your friend. But guilt doesn't fit the facts here—you didn't do anything to your friend by being a good athlete. Opposite action prevents you from leaving the team you love based on emotions that don't make sense for the situation.

122

PROBLEM SOLVING

First, we need to ask ourselves if the issue at hand is our problem to solve. Are we jumping in unasked? This can be tricky for neurodivergent people, who are very justice minded. You feel outrage whenever someone makes a joke about your Goth sister's appearance, and you want to do something about it. But it's good to take a pause and ask if she actually wants you to take action. She might not be bothered by it, or she might actually love shocking people. In other words, she might not even see it as a problem. And even if she does, she doesn't necessarily want you to solve it for her. Stop and ask your sister how you can support her.

If it is a problem that needs to be solved by you, you can follow these steps:

DESCRIBE THE PROBLEM, USING OBSERVE AND DESCRIBE SKILLS	Getting specific about the problem can help with identifying the solution. For example, if you identify the problem as "chemistry class just sucks," that doesn't give you as many paths to solving the problem as identifying that "My teacher moves on to new topics faster than I can keep up."
DESCRIBE ANY OBSTACLES TO SOLVING THE PROBLEM	Obstacles can be internal, like beliefs that "I should handle my problems on my own" or "it's embarrassing to ask for help." They can also be external, such as graduation requirements or deadlines for drop/add. The list of obstacles might seem overwhelming—but don't stop here!
CHECK THE FACTS	Is the class always this difficult, or is it a particular unit that you're having a hard time with? Do you have a 504 or IEP that could be modified to support your challenges in chemistry class? How is your teacher likely to respond if you ask them to repeat their explanation or even talk to them after class? Checking the facts helps ground in reality.

IDENTIFY YOUR GOAL	What is your goal? Is it completing chemistry class this year, so you have room next year to take computer programming? Or is your goal to reduce overwhelm, and whether you take chemistry now doesn't significantly affect long-term plans? Different goals point to different solutions. If you want to finish chemistry class, you might talk to your teacher about your concerns, seek tutoring, or look for YouTube channels that explain chemistry concepts. If you want less stress, you might talk to your school counselor about modifying your schedule.
BRAINSTORM SOLUTIONS TO ACHIEVING YOUR GOAL	Don't limit yourself to what seems achievable or realistic—put down every option you can think of. You might have an initial solution you think is the best, but this is a good exercise for developing more mental flexibility and building the skill of identifying different options. It's also an effective strategy for negotiating. You might decide that the only answer to this problem is that you be switched into a class with a different chemistry teacher, right now, but if that class is full, it may not be a real option. Having backup solutions can be helpful.
CHOOSE A SOLUTION AND TEST IT	Pretend you're a scientist. If you're torn between more than one solution, weigh the pros and cons of each. Which solution fits the facts, your goals, and your values the best?
EVALUATE HOW THE PROBLEM-SOLVING PROCESS WENT	Did you solve the problem in a way that worked for you? Solutions may not work because we forgot an aspect of the situation or an unexpected obstacle came up. What did work about the solution? Can you feel pride in trying to directly address a challenge?

OPPOSITE ACTION

Opposite action is helpful when your emotion does not fit the facts or when acting on your emotions is not likely to be effective. For example, you may find that you process information from audiobooks much more easily than you do from reading but feel shame about this and force yourself to read paper books. However, that shame about how you best take in information does not fit the facts—it is just a processing difference, not a character flaw. Though your feelings are real, opposite action here would guide you to go against shame and use audiobooks (which is also more effective for learning).

It's important to remember that even if your emotion doesn't fit the facts, that doesn't mean that you're "wrong" for having it. If your friends are planning a trip to the mall, and you decline because you find the mall overstimulating, it's still okay to feel sad when you see them posting pictures of their fun day. It would not fit the facts, however, to blame your friends for your sadness. After all, they asked and you declined (for good reason!). If your sadness is telling you to avoid your friends, you could try opposite action by texting them about something they posted. "I saw you got some more Magic cards, wanna play Tuesday?"

Similarly, in the example of having trouble with your chemistry class, it is valid to feel some fear about talking to your teacher. It's a vulnerable thing to say you need help. You might be worried that you're putting too much work on your teacher's plate. If you check the facts and see that your teacher is usually happy to re-explain something to the class, though, then intense fear would not fit the facts. Here, you could use opposite action by approaching your teacher.

On the other hand, if your teacher actually isn't that friendly, your fear better fits the facts. However, acting on fear by avoiding your struggles with the material is not likely to help you do better in the class. You may choose to address it with the teacher or talk to your guidance counselor. You may ask for support from a parent in advocating for yourself.

To engage in opposite action:

- **CONNECT WITH WISE MIND.** Doing so will help you see if acting on your emotion will fit your goals in this situation. It's important to remember that opposite action should only be engaged in after checking in with your wise mind. Many neurodivergent people have the experience of being told that their feelings and sensations are wrong and should always be overridden. You may doubt your own perceptions of situations and believe you always have to take the path of doing the uncomfortable thing. Sometimes we do have to handle discomfort, whether because it's actually necessary (such as tolerating ear drops for an ear infection) or because it's in the service of our goals. Growth is not always comfortable, especially if we tend to like certainty and routine, but it's often better for us in the long run—as long as it's growth in a direction that is meaningful to us. Take some time to sit with yourself before deciding whether you should try opposite action.

- **IDENTIFY WHAT YOUR EMOTIONS ARE PROMPTING YOU TO DO.** Is sadness telling you to avoid people? Guilt telling you to punish yourself? Anger urging you to yell at someone? What are some ways you can act opposite to these messages?

- **CHANGING YOUR PHYSICAL POSTURE.** This simple change can be a good way to start acting opposite, if you're not sure where to start. Referring to the chart in section 23 or your own understanding of how emotions affect your body, you can change your physical posture to begin counteracting your emotion. If guilt makes you hunch over and fold your arms in, try straightening your posture. If anger makes you clench your teeth and fists, try relaxing your jaw and hands.

- **ACT OPPOSITE ALL THE WAY.** If you're feeling sad, don't go on a walk and mope and complain the whole time—or at least, don't do that and expect it to change your mood! Instead, you might go for a walk and practice noticing when you're complaining. You can mentally note each thought as a complaint.

FOR YOU TO DO

Do you have a problem where you can practice applying problem-solving skills?
Remember that when practicing new skills, it's easier to begin with something that is not a crisis and does not trigger very high emotions. With that in mind, what problem can you apply your new skills to?

_____

Plan ahead—identify some ways you can act opposite when the following emotions arise but don't fit the facts:

ANGER	
FEAR	
SADNESS	
SHAME	
GUILT	
JEALOUSY	

SECTION 26
COPING THROUGH STRONG EMOTIONS

Emotions can come on suddenly and intensely. Really intense emotion makes it hard to think clearly. When in intense emotional states, it's hard to make the best decisions we can. When emotions are high, or a crisis occurs, we need to be able to take a break. DBT offers distress tolerance skills that allow us to get through hard situations without making things worse.

What sets off intense emotions or even a crisis varies from person to person. It's not helpful to judge yourself for what feels overwhelming to you.

Neurodivergent people are often prone to strong emotions. If you have alexithymia, you may not notice your feelings until they're very intense. If you're very values driven, it's hard to see those values violated. Neurodivergent folks often have ongoing sensory stressors and invalidation, and that makes us more vulnerable to having consuming emotional experiences.

Ari's best friend Andre is a little older and seems to think that means he knows better than Ari. Ari feels like Andre is bossier than his probation officer was. Ari gets a lot of enjoyment out of his particular clothing and cologne, and it irritates him when Andre makes comments about his appearance. Andre also tends to dictate what they do when they hang out. Ari tries to make a suggestion that they go out dancing this weekend, but Andre dismisses this. Ari feels rage when he gets Andre's text. He doesn't want to act on this rage, though—that's how he ended up on probation last year.

It's important to know that from a DBT perspective, the purpose is *not* to "get rid of your emotions." The actions that emotions urge us to take are sometimes necessary as well. These skills instead are meant to help you pause and cope through the strong emotions.

WHEN INTENSE EMOTIONS STRIKE

A first line of defense is the DBT skill known as TIPP. Like all skills, it's good to practice before you urgently need it. When you're in a mildly stressed state, you can try one or all of the following:

- **TEMPERATURE.** Cold water on your face activates the dive reflex, which slows heart rate—useful in a time of high stress. Fill a bowl with ice cold water and place your face in the water while holding your breath for fifteen to thirty seconds. You can also do this with an ice pack on your forehead.

- **INTENSE EXERCISE.** Exercise that works for your body is a quick way to get rid of some energy and help feel more grounded. Intense exercise is anything that elevates your heart rate. It can be brief—even ten or fifteen minutes is often enough to have a big impact. Go for a run, lift something heavy, or do some push-ups. (Regular exercise is a good ongoing practice to manage stress and boost your mood as well.)

- **PACED BREATHING.** Breathe in slowly through your nose, and exhale slowly through your mouth. Be sure to breathe out longer than you breathe in. You can try breathing in for the count of three and breathing out for the count of five. Experiment with what feels good for you.

- **PROGRESSIVE MUSCLE RELAXATION.** This is a great way to let go of tension in your body, and it can even help with falling asleep. Start by tensing up the muscles in your head and face for five seconds, then let them all go. Continue down through your body until you reach your feet, tensing them and then letting go. Finish this process by tensing all the muscles in your body for five seconds, and let all your muscles go.

Do not engage in these practices if they go against advice from your medical provider. These actions are all helpful right when the crisis or wave of emotion hits. They're not long-term solutions for a crisis, but they can help reduce emotion quickly and help you access wise mind to make better choices.

Ari goes for a run while listening to loud music. After twenty minutes, he is feeling much better. That night, he is thinking of Andre's text while trying to settle down to sleep. He does some progressive muscle relaxation to help him calm down.

FEEL YOUR FEELINGS

You may have heard the therapist advice to "feel your feelings." But what exactly does feeling your feelings look like, and why would you want to do it?

Feeling your feelings—or "mindfulness of current emotion," in DBT terms—is applying mindfulness skills to the emotions that are coming up for you. What thoughts do you notice? Are there any physical sensations or urges that arise? Do you feel called to take action? Don't try to change or direct these experiences, just observe them. Notice any shifts in intensity: Does the feeling get stronger as you sit with it? Does it fade away? The intensity may fluctuate.

Many of us recoil at the idea of sitting with emotions. Shame, guilt, anger, and sadness can be difficult to tolerate at all. Even happiness can feel risky and dangerous. But hiding away from our emotional experience doesn't make our emotions go away.

Avoiding emotions tends to spread beyond just the emotions we're trying to avoid. You may start off avoiding feelings of shame, but ignoring your internal world can mean that eventually, you stop noticing more pleasant emotions as well. Avoidance can be a good short-term strategy—if you just need to get through a presentation at school, putting aside your worry about your grandmother's health issues is an effective approach to doing your assignment. But avoidance over the long term tends to sensitize us to the emotion we're avoiding, and so it furthers more avoidance. It can take less and less of the emotion to trigger a strong response—and the impulse to escape into avoidance. This can look like avoiding your feelings of grief around the loss of a loved one, then becoming so sensitized to sadness that even something that would normally have made you feel mildly sad now causes intense panic and overwholm.

Feeling your feelings can help with learning to tolerate even unpleasant emotions and learning that emotion changes over time. What seemed unbearable becomes something you can cope through. Practicing this skill can also help with developing greater awareness of your emotions if you're alexithymic. It's easier to practice when you are not in extreme distress. A good time to practice might be when you are feeling a pleasant emotion or an emotion that is hard but not overwhelming.

EXERCISE FEEL YOUR FEELINGS

Steps to begin feeling your feelings:

1. Get to a place and in a position that allows you to focus on your internal world. You do not have to look like the cross-legged, eyes-closed stock image of a someone meditating. You can get in whatever position will help you focus best. Keep a fidget in your hand or play hip-hop music if that helps you focus better.
2. When you are ready to begin, focus on the thoughts that come up for you. Recognize them as thoughts, either by noting "that's a thought," or by restating, "I'm having the thought that my day will be ruined now."
3. Use observe and describe skills to notice bodily sensations.
4. Try to identify what emotion you are having. Your thoughts and physical sensations are important clues to your feeling.
5. Do not try to change the feeling by pushing it away or "solving" it. You are just practicing observing and describing what is happening. The feeling will likely shift over time, but do not force it.
6. Do not try to perpetuate the feeling either. If you find yourself adding to the reasons why you should feel the way you are feeling (for example, if you're sad, thinking about other things that have made you sad in the past or could make you sad in the future), focus on the here and now. The pain of this present moment is enough to bear.
7. Remember that no emotion lasts forever.

Even practicing this for a minute is helpful in becoming more comfortable with difficult emotions. Try feeling your feelings before you go on to use other skills. As with all the skills in this book, the more you practice them, the better you will be able to access them when you are in distress.

WHAT TO DO WHILE YOU WAIT FOR EMOTIONS TO CHANGE

The skill "Wise Mind ACCEPTS" outlines steps you can take while you're waiting for intense emotions to pass:

- **ACTIVITIES:** Fully engage in an activity to take your mind off what is upsetting you. This is a great time to turn to your special interests! You could also engage in soothing sensory activities. Revisit a book you loved or take a walk and notice the scenery.

- **CONTRIBUTING:** Step outside yourself. How can you help someone else? You might agree to help your sister with her homework. Stop by the school library and ask if there's any volunteer work to do.

- **COMPARISONS:** Some people find it helpful to compare how they are coping now versus how they coped when they had fewer skills or supports. You might remind yourself that you're now more aware of your neurodivergence and being kinder to yourself. If you used to get through hard times with risky coping strategies like self-harm or alcohol, celebrate that you're not doing that now.

- **EMOTIONS:** Take a vacation from your current emotions. Listen to a funny podcast to have a good laugh. If you're feeling numb, you might watch something that will provoke a strong response, like a scary movie.

- **PUSHING AWAY:** As a temporary strategy, don't allow yourself to think about the crisis. You could write about the situation and put it in an envelope marked "for later." You might set a picture of a brick wall as your phone lockscreen to remind you that this subject is off limits for now.

- **THOUGHTS:** Focus on one thing at a time. You might focus on a stimming behavior, sing along with a song you love, or count the number of round things you see in the space around you.

- **SENSATIONS:** Using sensory input that you find pleasant and invigorating can be helpful here. Sour candy, discordant music, or rolling spiky rubber balls under your feet might be a nice distraction.

Ari is still too upset to talk to Andre, so he focuses on using ACCEPTS skills. He tells the cashier at the corner store her tattoo is cool, which makes her happy (contributing). Ari reminds himself that "at least I'm not threatening anyone with a knife," like he did last year (comparisons). He spends an afternoon thrift shopping (activities) and wears a cologne that always makes him feel good (sensations).

It's helpful to write out some ideas for how you can use ACCEPTS, to have on hand for when you need it.

Radical acceptance (section 21) is another practice that helps with distress tolerance.

FOR YOU TO DO

Practice at least one of the TIPP skill activities. **What was it like? Can you imagine using it at a time of high stress?**

Practice feeling your feelings. Set a timer for two minutes and remember that it's normal for your attention to wander in mindfulness practice! What emotion did you observe? **What did you notice about the emotion over the course of the two minutes?**

Plan ahead for how you might use ACCEPTS. **Write out some ideas you could try to distract yourself the next time you feel overwhelmed by emotions and need to ride them out.**

ACTIVITIES	
CONTRIBUTING	

COMPARISONS	
EMOTIONS	
PUSHING AWAY	
THOUGHTS	
SENSATIONS	

SECTION 27
REJECTION SENSITIVITY

Rejection sensitivity (sometimes called rejection sensitivity dysphoria, or RSD) is the experience of feeling significant emotional pain due to rejection. It's commonly associated with ADHD, though other neurodivergent people report experiencing it as well. This rejection can be something that actually occurs, such as not being picked for a sports team. However, just the possibility of rejection can also trigger this response as well. Simply considering trying out for the team and imagining not making it could trigger RSD.

Most of us don't like being rejected! But rejection sensitivity is a whole other level of emotional pain. When rejection sensitivity hits, it can be intense. You might experience any of the following:

- intense shame

- wanting to hide

- humiliation

- suicidal thoughts

- self-harm urges

- avoidance

Suresh is an artist. He spends hours in his favorite chair, drawing scenes from his favorite books. Suresh dreams of being an illustrator for fantasy novels or even working on designs for TV shows or games. His mother knows about his interest in art and encourages him to sign up for art classes at school. Suresh spirals into panic at the thought of his work being critiqued. In fact, he's so afraid of people's feedback that only his mom and stepdad have seen his drawings.

Some people argue that being intensely sensitive to rejection is a natural response for neurodivergent people, who are often in fact rejected for their neurodivergent traits. After all, we live in a world that invalidates neurodivergence, which tells neurodivergent people in many subtle (and not subtle!) ways, over and over, that they are different.

This perspective can be helpful for some people: feeling sensitive to rejection is caused largely by an unfair world. From this perspective, one way to counter RSD would be to surround yourself with people and media that affirm you as a neurodivergent person.

HOW TO COPE WITH RSD

It's important to learn to manage rejection sensitivity as well as you can. First, it's a very distressing experience! Second, feedback is an important part of learning. If any potentially negative feedback feels world ending, that will make it difficult to take constructive criticism—which makes it harder to improve even at things you want to get better at.

Rejection sensitivity can also have negative effects on your relationships. It's hard for people to feel like if they turn down an invitation, the other person might experience suicidal feelings. Your friends may feel they can't be honest with you. Unspoken conflict can simmer. RSD is not something you "do" to people on purpose, *and* it still affects how people respond to you. Navigating rejection sensitivity can help improve all aspects of your life.

How do you cope with rejection sensitivity? First, being aware that rejection sensitivity is something you are prone to is helpful. If you're able to name what is happening, it can help create a bit of distance between your thoughts and emotions.

The skills in the section "Coping Through Strong Emotions" can be useful. Write these skills down and have them somewhere accessible since it's hard to remember skills in the heat of the moment. You can even take a picture and use it as the lock screen on your phone or keep a list in your wallet. If there are people you can trust, you can confide in them that you experience RSD, and they can help remind you of the skills to use. If rejection sensitivity is causing significant problems in your life, it may be useful to speak to a mental health professional.

Some people find it helpful to use affirmations. These are positive self-statements—things you say to yourself, out loud or in your head. You might remind yourself that it's okay to not be perfect, that a relationship is more than one hard moment, or simply that your feelings make sense given what is happening.

Others find it helpful to connect to their values. For example, the thought of applying for jobs might be terrifying, but the need for the security that money can bring might override your feelings about being rejected for jobs.

Plan ahead for times you know you are likely to experience rejection sensitivity. How can you give yourself time and space to recover?

Suresh has been watching interviews with professional artists on the realities of their careers. Despite the struggles that would come with being a working artist, Suresh still finds the prospect exciting. He realizes that he needs to be able to show his work to others. He reminds himself that his most important value for a career is creativity. He asks around for the name of the nicest art teacher at his school and makes an appointment to talk to her and show her his work. Suresh knows that whatever she says, it's likely to be hard. He and his mom plan to have a call right after the meeting, and Suresh plans to reread a favorite graphic novel that night. It's a good vacation from the intensity of his feelings. Even while his feelings are overwhelming, Suresh reminds himself that he is being brave by sharing his artwork.

FOR YOU TO DO

Do you experience rejection sensitivity? Are there situations that are more likely to set it off? What have you tried to help cope with it?

Identify an upcoming situation that may activate rejection sensitivity. Identify three things you can do ahead of time to mitigate the impacts.

PART 5

COMMUNICATION AND RELATIONSHIPS

SECTION 28

NEURODIVERGENT COMMUNICATION IN A NEUROTYPICAL WORLD

Communication can be challenging for everyone, but it's often especially tricky for neurodivergent people. This is usually framed as a problem with the neurodivergent person; for example, "persistent deficits" in communication are part of the DSM criteria for autism. However, more recent research describes what is called the "double empathy problem." Researchers paired up people as follows:

- two autistic people

- two allistic people

- one autistic person and one allistic person

Researchers found that communication was fairly smooth in the all-autistic group and the all-allistic group. That is, the autistic folks didn't have "communication deficits" in a group of their neurotype—same as the allistic-only group. It was the mixed-neurotype group that had the most communication breakdowns. This indicates that neurotypical and neurodivergent communication challenges are more like the differences you would find in communication between teenagers and adults. Each group may struggle to understand the cultural references the other group makes or even the way they communicate (preferring phone calls instead of texting, for example). Neither group is right or wrong— just different. Reframing neurodivergent communication differences this way can help reduce any shame you may feel about how you communicate with or understand others.

Here are some common neurodivergent communication experiences; check off any that apply to you:

- [ ] Talking to discuss a specific topic or task rather than talking for the sake of socializing. When the info about the task has been given or the conversation moves on from the initial topic, you may be uninterested in continuing.

- [ ] "Infodumping," or talking at length about a subject that interests you. This subject may connect to what someone else said, or it may not.

- [ ] Offering a lot of context and complexity. You may not feel comfortable making blanket statements without acknowledging exceptions to the rule.

- [ ] Being direct about your opinions. Observing social hierarchies (paying respect to someone simply because they are older) or "softening" your language may be difficult or seem irrelevant.

- [ ] Not contributing to the conversation if you don't have anything to share.

- [ ] Being literal and taking statements at face value—even if you're also capable of sarcasm, picking up on others' sarcasm can be difficult.

- [ ] Losing focus in long conversations or being easily distracted.

Here are some communication styles and experiences that tend to be common for neurotypical people. Check off any that apply to you:

- [ ] Using nonverbal cues to convey meaning or change the meaning of their words; for example, winking to indicate playfulness or a joke.

- [ ] Enjoyment in a conversation may be in spending time getting to know the other person rather than sharing information. The subject may be secondary or even irrelevant to this social goal.

☐ An unspoken expectation of reciprocity. For example, thinking everyone should take up roughly the same amount of time speaking.

☐ Making statements that indirectly invite follow up. Someone might say "I'm really looking forward to the weekend!" with the expectation that they will be asked, "Oh, are you doing anything cool?"

☐ Speaking in a conversation is seen as a sign of interest, even if it is a comment that does not add new information or deepen the conversation. ("Homework is such a drag!")

You may have characteristics associated with each group. This doesn't mean you aren't neurodivergent. It can be simply other cultural differences. Gender, age, and race are just a few of the identities that influence how we are expected to communicate. It can also mean that you are engaging in a lot of masking in social situations. Again, at times this is adaptive, but masking all the time can lead to burnout.

IMPROVING COMMUNICATION

Understanding some of these communication differences can help improve your understanding of others *and* yourself. Even if you are in a situation where you are not able to make requests around changing communication, knowing that you are not inherently wrong for the way you communicate reduces self-blame.

Being able to speak openly about communication differences is ideal. If you can explain that you don't always get jokes the first time because you tend to take things literally, it can help other people understand that might be why you're not laughing—not that you're saying they're unfunny.

Use observe and describe skills to clarify what is unclear to you. Instead of saying, "I don't understand," be more descriptive and ask, "When you say, 'You could stack the chairs,' are you saying that I should stack the chairs or that it's optional?"

Practice being nonjudgmental, both about your own communication style and the communication styles of others. Patience and curiosity may take longer, but they're more effective for communication. Relationships ideally involve both people understanding and working with each other's communication styles—whether you have the same neurotype or not.

It is unfair to expect neurodivergent people to always meet the norms of neurotypical people. If you are always bending to meet the other person, it's not an equal relationship. At the same time, it is not useful to assume that neurotypical people (or even other neurodivergent people!) are aware of the work you are doing to meet communication norms. If someone finds small talk easy, they may never consider someone else would struggle. Approaching communication as a collaborative conversation is more effective.

FOR YOU TO DO

Is there a communication norm that causes a lot of challenges for you? What are a few ways you could address this, without having to mask?

Are there people you find it easier to communicate with? Identify three things that make communication with these people smoother.

SECTION 29

SHARING YOUR NEURODIVERGENCE

Neurodivergence has long been considered something that should be hidden. Being different is often seen as concerning or even bad. Thankfully, we are moving into a more affirming world. As you come to understand yourself and your neurodivergence, you may want to share your discoveries.

Of course, you may not always have the choice of whether to tell people about your neurodivergence. If you have an official diagnosis, your immediate family and medical professionals will know. Teachers and staff will know if you have a 504 or IEP. They will also know details about the supports you need to succeed at school. You have the right to attend these meetings and share your input with the school team.

With friends, extended family, coworkers, and other people, it is optional to share your neurodivergence. Here are a few reasons you might do so:

- **PRIDE IN WHO YOU ARE.** Like any other part of your identity, you may want to celebrate your neurodivergence. You might wear pins for neurodivergent pride or casually mention your identities in conversation. Expressing pride can be a powerful form of validation.

- **NORMALIZING NEURODIVERGENCE.** Many people still have misconceptions about neurodivergence, such as that it is rare or "obvious." You may want to speak up to remind people that neurodivergent people are everywhere. Sharing your neurodivergence can make it easier for others to advocate for their needs as well.

- **GETTING ACCESS TO SERVICES AND SUPPORTS.** Whether or not you have a formal diagnosis, you may seek accommodations at school or work. You may need to explain why you need these supports, or you may not. Some teachers, for example, are fine with students listening to music on headphones while they do quiet work and do not need a "reason" to grant that request.

- **INCREASE UNDERSTANDING.** Neurodivergent behavior is often misunderstood when judged by neurotypical standards. For example, maintaining eye contact is considered a way of showing that you are paying attention. You may choose to explain that you find it easier to listen when you're not making eye contact, so your friends understand that you are still listening.

THINGS TO CONSIDER

Disclosing should be done when it feels good for you or when it's necessary to access supports and services you would like. No one else can decide for you when you should be "out" as neurodivergent. There may be safety considerations you have to make. If you are in a very hostile environment, you might make very strategic choices about disclosing.

Eliot was identified as autistic at age nine. He likes to tell his teachers at the beginning of the year that he is autistic and what that means in their class. He shares that he struggles with open-ended assignments and might need help narrowing down what is being asked in an assignment. He also lets his teachers know that he generally will not look at them but that he is paying attention.

If you feel nervous talking about neurodivergence, consider practicing with a friendly person first. This could be someone you are already close with or someone who shows signs of being an open and affirming person. The teacher who allows students to get up and walk around the class as needed, or who is okay with snacking or fidgets, might be a good person to talk to. You might choose to speak with a teacher privately. Look for someone who displays neurodiversity-affirming signs, such as the rainbow infinity symbol. You can use therapy as a space to practice having conversations that you feel worried about. School counselors can be a helpful resource as well.

You may disclose a particular label or identity, or disclose just your specific need. You might say, "I can be really literal, so I'm not sure if that's a joke," or, "I could really use step-by-step instructions on this."

When disclosing, it's worth thinking about what it is you want the other person to understand. If you are sharing your neurodivergence simply as a matter of pride, you might stop at "I'm dyslexic." But if there is something particular you want the other person to understand, you need to be more specific. Simply saying "I have PTSD" or "I am an ADHDer" does not give any information about what that means for *you*. Those experiences vary a lot, and what works for one person with PTSD may not work for another. Some autistic people are very sensitive to sound, and others are completely unbothered by it. You need to be clear in your communication. In our example with Eliot, he shares specific information so his teachers can better understand him. It's helpful not to assume others have the same knowledge about neurodivergence that you do.

FOR YOU TO DO

Have you disclosed your neurodivergence to anyone? How did you decide to do so?

What do you want others to know about your neurodivergence?

Who would be a good person to share this info with?

SECTION 30

BOUNDARIES

Boundaries are the limits we set with others about how we would like to be treated. You can set boundaries around your time, your physical space, your money, or any other aspect of your life.

Some examples of boundaries:

- not wanting to watch movies with violent scenes

- asking for a text before someone shows up at your house

- not hanging out with people when they're drunk

- staying in the night before a test to get a good night's sleep

- requiring your partner to use a condom

Your own boundaries may shift over time or be different in different relationships. You might not want feedback about your artwork from most people but be okay with it coming from your favorite teacher. You may be more private at one point in your life and later be more open about your thoughts, feelings, and experiences.

Different people have different boundaries—and that's fine! Some people may judge your boundaries as too rigid or too loose. Only you get to say what your boundaries are and whether they work for you. For example, if you have pretty open boundaries around personal information and find yourself repeatedly hurt because of this, you can weigh if you want to be more cautious (stricter boundaries). Or you may decide that openness is a core value of yours and continue to share a lot with people.

If your boundaries aren't working for you, it's worth examining what is getting in your way. Are you clear on your boundaries? What are your fears about expressing them and enforcing them? What responses have you gotten when you have expressed boundaries in the past?

HOW TO EXPRESS BOUNDARIES

You can express boundaries directly, such as telling someone their jokes are offensive to you. You can also indirectly communicate by rolling your eyes or not laughing at the joke. Over time, you might stop hanging out with that friend.

Indirect expression may fit better with some cultures. It may simply be more comfortable for some people. Direct expression of a boundary is clearer, however. In the case of an offensive joke, the friend might simply think you're not laughing because they didn't tell the joke well. They might not realize the subject matter is the problem. There's no one "right way" to set a boundary. When it comes to setting boundaries, it's about what feels doable—and what's effective.

Setting boundaries is a way to express your needs. Even if other people don't understand or even respect your boundaries, standing up for yourself is a way to validate your needs. Avoid apologizing for your boundary. There's nothing wrong with asserting your needs.

Boundaries need to have clear consequences. For example, if you tell someone that you won't hang out with them if they keep making jokes about fat people but you continue to hang out with them, you are not holding your own boundary. It is up to us to enforce our boundaries. If others don't remember or respect our boundaries, it's our job to remind them. You might make decisions about if and how you continue in the relationship going forward.

Judah is a self-described "neurosparkly" seventeen-year-old who is alexithymic. He knows that he takes a while to identify his feelings. He also has a tendency to give an automatic "no" to changes in plans or new ideas. While he's working on increasing his emotional awareness and cognitive flexibility, Judah also knows that to some degree, this is likely to be a challenge for him. When he has tried to compensate for his automatic "no" by giving an automatic "yes," Judah has ended up doing things he later realizes he was never interested in. Judah has accepted that he needs time—time to recognize his feelings, time to let the intensity of the automatic "no" fade, and time to access wise mind. He's told his friends that if they pressure him to make a quick decision, his answer is likely going to be no, because he wants to avoid saying yes to something without full consideration. If his friends want him to make a decision right now, he reminds them that he doesn't work well under pressure. He does have one exception to his "no pressure rule"—if one of his friends is in urgent need, he will be there to help them. Judah's strong values around community and friendship allow him to overcome his need for deliberation when his neighbor texts Judah to pick her up from a date that is getting uncomfortable.

Judah's knowledge about his tendencies and the way his neurodivergence has shown up has allowed him to set boundaries to support the way he processes information. At the same time, Judah's awareness of his values lets him override these tendencies in an urgent situation. Judah has created boundaries that support both his values and his own needs.

FOR YOU TO DO

When is it easy for you to set boundaries? When is it hard?

Are there boundaries you would like to set? What are they?

Identify two boundaries you can practice setting and write a plan for how you can implement them.

SECTION 31
NAVIGATING CONFLICT

The idea of conflict often makes people uneasy. This can be especially true if you're a neurodivergent person who has learned to "people please" to find connection or because you have been criticized for being "too difficult." Conflict can also be scary if you have a history of exploding with anger. It can feel like even going toward conflict can be dangerous. But conflict does not cease to exist because we ignore it. Boundary violations and conflicting values will continue to exist, and by avoiding them, you run the risk of things blowing up in an unskilled way when you can't handle them anymore. It is more effective to approach conflict from a regulated, wise-minded place.

People often fear that conflict will destroy relationships, and truthfully, it may lead to the end of a relationship. But research shows us that successfully handling conflict together in fact strengthens relationships. Think about it: Would you rather be friends with someone you can be honest with or someone you have to walk on eggshells with? Being able to have conflict is a sign of the strength of the connection.

Other times, risking conflict may feel necessary because that conflict is in line with your values. If you don't stand up for a classmate who is being bullied, you might feel like you've let yourself down. Speaking up for what is important to you helps increase your own self-respect. Even if you feel little hope that you will change your classmates' minds on gun control, you might feel bad about yourself if you don't speak up.

When you notice tension or conflict brewing, or you notice a boundary of yours has been violated, use your skills to determine whether you need to move into problem solving. If you are generally avoidant of speaking up or addressing tension, consider whether it's time to use opposite action skills to approach the thing you want to avoid.

Sometimes making a request can be as simple as saying, "Don't call me Willie anymore. I like Will better." Other times, we might need or want to give more info. DBT offers a step-by-step guide to assert boundaries or make requests of people in general. This skill is called DEARMAN, and the letters spell out the process of making a request:

- **DESCRIBE:** Use nonjudgmental language to describe a situation.

- **EXPRESS:** Name your emotions simply as facts. Don't ascribe responsibility to another person, such as by saying, "You made me mad." Instead, say, "I'm mad."

- **ASSERT:** Clearly state your request.

- **REINFORCE:** You can tell the other person why they should meet your request. You can also "reward" someone by thanking them or offering appreciation when they are supportive of your request.

- **MINDFUL:** Stay focused on your goal. Use the "broken record" technique to repeat your request. Don't get sidetracked by other issues.

- **APPEAR:** Appear confident, even if you're nervous inside. A straight posture usually shows more confidence than being slumped over. Don't undercut your request by saying things like "I know I'm probably making a big deal out of nothing" or apologizing for having a need.

- **NEGOTIATE:** Know if the request is something you would be willing to be flexible about. If so, how much can you compromise? You may also not be willing to compromise at all on certain subjects.

Ari is frustrated with his best friend, Andre. He feels Andre is always bossing him around and telling him what to do. After coping through his intense feelings about this (see section 26), Ari has decided he can say something to Andre from his wise mind.

DESCRIBE	"Andre, the last ten times we've hung out, you have decided what we're doing. I have tried to offer suggestions, but you just say no or ignore what I've said."
EXPRESS	"It's really frustrating. I want to decide what we do sometimes too. I am really tired of you always deciding things."
ASSERT	"I want to pick what we do next weekend."
REINFORCE	"If you don't let me pick what we do, I'm not going to hang out with you on Friday. I might not want to hang out with you, period."
MINDFUL	When Andre starts to say that he "just knows about cooler stuff to do" than Ari does, Ari just repeats, "I want to pick what we do next weekend."
APPEAR	Ari does not apologize to Andre about wanting to make the plans for Friday. He doesn't overexplain what he is thinking.
NEGOTIATE	When Andre reminds Ari that they already bought movie tickets for Friday, Ari says, "Okay, but then I get to pick what we do the next two times."

Reflecting on the DEARMAN process before you make a request can be a helpful way to get clear on your emotions and boundaries.

FOR YOU TO DO

Practice using DEARMAN.

Situation:

DESCRIBE	
EXPRESS	
ASSERT	
REINFORCE	
MINDFUL	
APPEAR	
NEGOTIATE	

What thoughts or feelings come up as you go through this exercise?

Can you imagine using it in real life? What challenges might get in the way of you using this skill?

SECTION 32
VALIDATING OTHERS

In section 10, we discussed self-validation and why it's important. Validating others is also a useful skill to have. It can help deepen your relationships. It can also help you handle conflicts more smoothly. If others feel heard by you seeing their perspective, they often feel closer to you.

Validation may involve agreeing with someone, but it doesn't have to. Imagine your friend is very sensitive to sudden loud noises. You don't need to have a problem with sudden loud noises to acknowledge that they're unpleasant for your friend.

It might feel impossible to validate something unless you think it's correct. DBT also has a saying to not "validate the invalid." This means that there are some things we simply can't validate. You can't support a friend saying they "should be thrown in the garbage" when they fail a quiz. But you can validate that your friend is in pain. We can also validate that those thoughts and feelings are reflecting your friend's experience.

In DBT, there are six levels of validation you can offer:

1. **PAY ATTENTION.** Give your attention to the other person. While you might draw or use a fidget to focus better, it means no multitasking—not trying to do your homework or reply to texts while someone is talking to you.

2. **REFLECT BACK.** Check that you heard what the other person is communicating, to be sure you are understanding them. Use a nonjudgmental tone. This is not the time to try and change the other person's mind—you're just checking for understanding. Be open to the other person correcting you.

160

If you're not sure, you can also check if the other person is being sincere or sarcastic.

3. **LOOK FOR THE UNSPOKEN.** Are there things the other person is expressing with their face or body posture? For example, if someone says, "No, it's cool," but has tears in their eyes, you can acknowledge what they might be expressing with their tears. You might say something like "It seems like you're upset." You might also just stand close to them, quietly offering support with your presence.

4. **SHOW YOU UNDERSTAND.** Reflect how your friend's response makes sense given their past or their state of mind: "You've already had a crappy day and now this happened. It makes sense why you're mad." "This cafeteria *is* hella loud." Again, this does not mean you're endorsing all of their views, just saying they make sense.

5. **ACKNOWLEDGE WHAT'S VALID.** Look for the kernel of truth, even if it is small. You might normalize their feelings by saying something like "I think most people would be upset about that."

6. **BE GENUINE.** Show up as a real human being who is talking to an equal. One way that neurodivergent people often validate others is by sharing their own similar experiences. Depending on the person, they might want to hear a little about your experience ("Oh, I was so bummed when my sister moved out. I know it sucks when your family changes like that."), or they might want to hear a lot. This kind of validation can also connect back to level 4, showing you understand.

Sometimes, it can be stressful to validate others because we're afraid of getting it wrong. While some people may be angry if we misunderstand them, a genuine attempt to connect is often well received—even if we get it wrong.

PUTTING VALIDATION INTO ACTION

It's easy to validate someone who is feeling sad or angry about a situation that doesn't involve us. It gets harder when someone is upset with something we did. However, that's often when validation is most useful.

Jenny is a fifteen-year-old gifted ADHDer. Her English teacher has paired the students up to do presentations to the class on a classic American novel. The presentation is in two weeks, and Jenny keeps putting off meeting with her partner because it feels far away. Two days before the presentation, she reaches out to her partner, who's upset because he has already done a lot of the work since he couldn't get hold of Jenny. Jenny feels bad and wants to smooth things over with her partner, and she also wants to be able to work together to finish the presentation.

Let's see how Jenny might use each of the levels of validation to improve her relationship with her presentation partner.

LEVEL OF VALIDATION	EXAMPLE
1: PAY ATTENTION	When Jenny realizes her partner is upset, she puts her phone away and gives him her attention. She hugs herself because the pressure helps her stay more present.
2: REFLECT BACK	Jenny says, "Since I didn't get back to you, you started doing it yourself. You've done most of the PowerPoint already." This helps her clarify that she is getting everything her partner is saying.
3: LOOK FOR THE UNSPOKEN	Jenny's partner hasn't directly expressed his feelings, but he's speaking in a flat tone that is different from his normal voice. Jenny ventures a guess: "I bet you're pretty annoyed with me."

4: SHOW YOU UNDERSTAND	Jenny continues: "It totally makes sense you're mad, I've been putting you off, and you've done like 75 percent of the work."
5: ACKNOWLEDGE WHAT'S VALID	"It would be really frustrating to not hear from me for like two weeks. I would be mad too."
6: BE GENUINE	Jenny might say, "Thank you for doing so much on this project. I'm sorry I didn't help."

Remember that we don't validate the invalid. If Jenny's partner had called her names or put her down, Jenny could validate his feeling of anger, but not his approach. "I get that you're upset with me. I would be too. But it's not cool to tell me I'm a loser."

Validating other people's experiences can help prevent polarization. That's where two people become stuck on opposite sides of an argument. If Jenny were to respond to her partner by saying, "What's the big deal? It's not even due for two more days. Lighten up!" it would probably only annoy her partner more. He might get more intense to prove his point to Jenny, which would likely make it harder for them to work together well.

You can think of polarization as playing tug-of-war. The harder one side pulls, the harder the other side pulls. Validation is like leaning in a bit toward the other person. It creates a little slack in the rope. Being the first person to lean in is a brave thing to do. Many people are resistant to loosening their end of the rope, but it is often more effective than continuing to dig in your heels.

FOR YOU TO DO

Find a situation in your life where validating another person would be helpful for your relationship or for meeting a goal.

LEVEL OF VALIDATION	EXAMPLE
1: PAY ATTENTION	
2: REFLECT BACK	
3: LOOK FOR THE UNSPOKEN	
4: SHOW YOU UNDERSTAND	
5: ACKNOWLEDGE WHAT'S VALID	
6: BE GENUINE	

Does the thought of validating people even if you disagree with them feel challenging? If so, why do you think that is?

FINDING YOUR NEXT STEPS:
LIVING THE LIFE YOU WANT

Now that you've made your way through this book, you've learned a lot about neurodivergence, DBT skills, and most importantly, yourself. Here are some reflection questions to help you identify goals for both the short and long term.

What are some things you have learned about your neurodivergence?

What information would you like to share with your family? Your friends?

Are there aspects of your neurodivergence that you want to follow up on? This could include:

- a deeper dive into a particular type of neurodivergence

- psychological or medical supports

- strategies for navigating your environment

- increasing sensory supports

- increasing self-acceptance

- finding neurodivergent-affirming community

Reflect on the goal of DBT: to help you build a life worth living—and that you are the only one who determines what that looks like. **What do you envision in your life worth living? If you feel challenged by this, think about some good experiences you have had that you definitely want more of. What do you notice about these experiences? Are there any common threads?**

What will your daily life look like? Will you live alone or with others? What would be your ideal physical environment? You can imagine this as in depth as you like! "I wake up in a bed covered with all of my rescue cats..."

How does your life worth living reflect your values?

Remember that building your life worth living doesn't mean that your life will be easy or perfect or that it will always go the way you want it to. **What challenges do you anticipate as you work toward your life worth living? What skills in this book can help you with those challenges?**

Knowing that skills are only built through practice, what skills do you want to focus on practicing regularly, as a first step?

ACKNOWLEDGMENTS

Thank you to my clients. You have been my greatest teachers, and I'm grateful to have gotten to work with you.

I've been blessed with a wonderful community of colleagues and mentors. Crystal Blanton, Noah Dzuba, Nikki Juanson, and David Khalili have been there since the beginning. Alison Nightingale always adds complexity to my clinical thinking, and Megan Stonelake is the best sounding board I could have asked for. Sonia Beers started this all. Itzel Molina keeps me from getting too polarized. Sarah DeMulder's cheerleading was essential. Megan Anna Neff, Sara Schmidt, and Lorie Rischtel have all shaped my thinking about DBT work with neurodivergent people—and have been graciously supportive as well. Kathryn Solie inspires me in so many ways, not least in the ways she challenges the limits we often accept around sensitivity. Kae Hixson's mentorship has radically changed and enlivened my work.

Thanks also to Jess O'Brien and the team at New Harbinger for all the encouragement and close reading. It's been a pleasure.

Thanks to the Kardokas-Johansons—Laima, Alan, Damien, and Eva—for their enthusiasm and interest in this book. Mom, thank you for your unending support. I know Dad would have been proud.

Ryder and Ragnar, our family is the foundation of my life worth living. I love you.

BIBLIOGRAPHY

Aron, E. 1997. *The Highly Sensitive Person: How to Thrive When the World Overwhelms You.* New York: Broadway Books.

Dunkley, C. 2020. *Regulating Emotion the DBT Way: A Therapist's Guide to Opposite Action.* New York: Routledge.

Forbes, K. 2020. "Home." Intune Pathways. https://www.kristyforbes.com.au.

Linehan, M. 2015a. *DBT Skills Training Handouts and Worksheets.* New York: The Guilford Press.

Linehan, M. 2015b. *DBT Skills Training Manual.* 2nd ed. New York: The Guilford Press.

Lo, I. 2018. *Emotional Sensitivity and Intensity: How to Manage Intense Emotions as a Highly Sensitive Person.* London: Hodder & Stoughton.

Mahler, K. 2019. "Home." Kelly Mahler. https://www.kelly-mahler.com.

Neff, M. A. 2021. *Insights of a Neurodivergent Clinician.* https://neurodivergentinsights.com.

Walker, N. 2018. *Neuroqueer: The Writings of Dr. Nick Walker.* https://neuroqueer.com.

Wise, S. J. 2022. *The Neurodivergent Friendly Workbook of DBT Skills.* Lived Experience Educator.

Rhiannon Theurer, LMFT, is a neurodivergent therapist in private practice who works with neurodivergent teens and adults. She earned her master's degree in counseling psychology from the Wright Institute in Berkeley, CA, and has worked in a variety of settings—from crisis lines to integrated clinics to schools (K-12). She lives in Ashland, OR.

Foreword writer **Megan Anna Neff, PsyD**, (she/they) is a neurodivergent psychologist and founder of Neurodivergent Insights, where she creates education and wellness resources for neurodivergent adults. Neff is the author of *Self-Care for Autistic People*.

More Instant Help Books for Teens
An Imprint of New Harbinger Publications

THE SHYNESS AND SOCIAL ANXIETY WORKBOOK FOR TEENS, SECOND EDITION

CBT and ACT Skills to Help You Build Social Confidence

978-1684038015 / US $23.95

THE HIGHLY SENSITIVE TEEN

Using Your Hidden Powers to Balance Emotions, Set Boundaries, and Embrace Who You Are

978-1648484032 / US $19.95

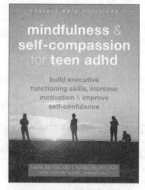

MINDFULNESS AND SELF-COMPASSION FOR TEEN ADHD

Build Executive Functioning Skills, Increase Motivation, and Improve Self-Confidence

978-1684036394 / US $16.95

THE ADHD WORKBOOK FOR TEENS

Activities to Help You Gain Motivation and Confidence

978-1572248656 / US $20.95

STUFF THAT'S LOUD

A Teen's Guide to Unspiraling When OCD Gets Noisy

978-1684035366 / US $19.95

THE AUTISM PLAYBOOK FOR TEENS

Imagination-Based Mindfulness Activities to Calm Yourself, Build Independence, and Connect with Others

978-1626250093 / US $20.95

newharbingerpublications

1-800-748-6273 / newharbinger.com

(VISA, MC, AMEX / prices subject to change without notice)

Follow Us

Don't miss out on new books from New Harbinger.
Subscribe to our email list at **newharbinger.com/subscribe**

Rhiannon Theurer, LMFT, is a neurodivergent therapist in private practice who works with neurodivergent teens and adults. She earned her master's degree in counseling psychology from the Wright Institute in Berkeley, CA, and has worked in a variety of settings—from crisis lines to integrated clinics to schools (K-12). She lives in Ashland, OR.

Foreword writer **Megan Anna Neff, PsyD**, (she/they) is a neurodivergent psychologist and founder of Neurodivergent Insights, where she creates education and wellness resources for neurodivergent adults. Neff is the author of *Self-Care for Autistic People*.

More Instant Help Books for Teens
An Imprint of New Harbinger Publications

THE SHYNESS AND SOCIAL ANXIETY WORKBOOK FOR TEENS, SECOND EDITION

CBT and ACT Skills to Help You Build Social Confidence

978-1684038015 / US $23.95

THE HIGHLY SENSITIVE TEEN

Using Your Hidden Powers to Balance Emotions, Set Boundaries, and Embrace Who You Are

978-1648484032 / US $19.95

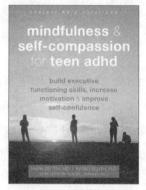

MINDFULNESS AND SELF-COMPASSION FOR TEEN ADHD

Build Executive Functioning Skills, Increase Motivation, and Improve Self-Confidence

978-1684036394 / US $16.95

THE ADHD WORKBOOK FOR TEENS

Activities to Help You Gain Motivation and Confidence

978-1572248656 / US $20.95

STUFF THAT'S LOUD

A Teen's Guide to Unspiraling When OCD Gets Noisy

978-1684035366 / US $19.95

THE AUTISM PLAYBOOK FOR TEENS

Imagination-Based Mindfulness Activities to Calm Yourself, Build Independence, and Connect with Others

978-1626250093 / US $20.95

newharbingerpublications
1-800-748-6273 / newharbinger.com

(VISA, MC, AMEX / prices subject to change without notice)

Follow Us

Don't miss out on new books from New Harbinger.
Subscribe to our email list at **newharbinger.com/subscribe**